GEOFFREY CHAUCER

Covering one of the most fascinating yet misunderstood periods in history, the MEDIEVAL LIVES series presents medieval people, concepts and events, drawing on political and social history, philosophy, material culture (art, architecture and archaeology) and the history of science. These books are global and wide-ranging in scope, encompassing both Western and non-Western subjects, and span the fifth to the fifteenth centuries, tracing significant developments from the collapse of the Roman Empire onwards.

SERIES EDITOR: Deirdre Jackson

GEOFFREY CHAUCER

Unveiling the Merry Bard

MARY FLANNERY

REAKTION BOOKS

For Helen Cooper and Colin Wilcockson, with all my thanks

Published by Reaktion Books Ltd
Unit 32, Waterside
44–48 Wharf Road
London N1 7UX, UK
www.reaktionbooks.co.uk

First published 2024
Copyright © Mary Flannery 2024

Printed and bound in India by Replika Press Pvt. Ltd

A catalogue record for this book is available from the British Library

ISBN 978 1 78914 863 3

CONTENTS

Important sites of 14th-century England and its environs.

ONE

The Merry Bard

Long had our dull Fore-Fathers slept Supine
Nor felt the Raptures of the tuneful Nine;
Till *Chaucer* first, a merry *Bard*, arose;
And many a Story told in Rhime and Prose.
JOSEPH ADDISON, 'TO MR. H. S[ACHEVEREL] APRIL 3, 1694'[1]

In a room not far from Westminster Abbey, a man lies on his deathbed. Approaching sixty years of age, he has lived what many people in the year 1400 would have judged to be a long life. It has also been a colourful life, one that led him from the comfortable merchant household of his early childhood to an adulthood spent in the service of English royalty. He has travelled a great deal, visiting not only some of the great houses of medieval England, but great cities in France, Italy, Spain and Flanders, among other places. He has performed a wide variety of jobs in the service of the recently deposed king, jobs related to diplomacy, customs, forestry, construction and jurisprudence. And he has managed to survive that king's deposition with his own career more or less intact – the new king, Henry IV, had on his coronation day granted him the yearly sum of 40 marks for life.[2]

But none of this is on his mind now. Here on his deathbed, he is instead plagued by guilt, shame and worry. True, he has not been convicted of any great crime, but what he has done is

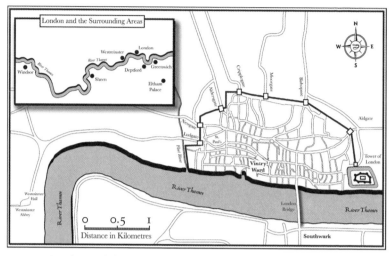

London and the surrounding areas.

perhaps worse, since its consequences will be more enduring: he has written many poems 'about the evil and most base love of men toward women'.[3] Time and time again, he cries out in torment: 'Woe is me, woe is me, because I will not be able now to call back or do away with those things . . . they will still continue to pass from person to person willy-nilly.'[4]

Soon thereafter, he breathes his last.

* * *

This is one fifteenth-century account of the imagined deathbed lamentations of medieval England's greatest poet: Geoffrey Chaucer (c. 1342–1400). The description of Chaucer's tormented mind appears in the writings of Thomas Gascoigne (1404–1458), a theologian and chancellor of the University of Oxford who was born four years after Chaucer's death. While it is possible that his description is based on a reliable source, most scholars believe it to be derived in large part from the words of Chaucer's own 'Retractions', an apparently remorseful text appended to some manuscript copies of his most famous work, *The Canterbury Tales*. In these 'Retractions', Chaucer addresses his readers directly:

> I biseke yow mekely, for the mercy of God, that ye preye for me that Crist have mercy on me and foryeve me my giltes;/ and namely of my translacions and enditynges of worldly vanitees, the whiche I revoke in my retracciouns:/ as is the book of Troilus; the book also of Fame; the book of the xxv. Ladies; the book of the Duchesse; the book of Seint Valentynes day of the Parlement of Briddes; the tales of Caunterbury, thilke that sownen into synne; the book of the Leoun; and many another book . . . and many a song and many a leccherous lay[.]

> I beseech you meekly, for the mercy of God, that you pray for me that Christ have mercy on me and forgive me my guilts, and namely for my translations and compositions of worldly vanities, which I revoke in my retractions: such as

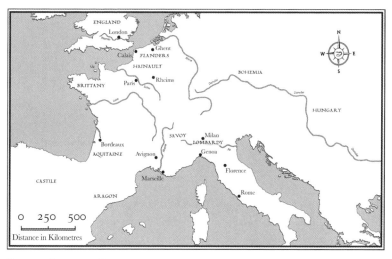

Fourteenth-century Europe.

the book of Troilus; also the book of Fame; the book of the
twenty-five Ladies; the book of the Duchess; the book of
Saint Valentine's Day of the Parliament of Birds; the tales
of Canterbury, those which concern sin; the book of the
Lion; and many another book . . . and many a song and
many a lecherous poem.[5]

It is difficult to know what to make of Chaucer's supposed
renunciation of his 'enditynges of worldly vanitees', particularly
since they include most of his best-known and best-loved works.
Was Chaucer really so ashamed and guilt-ridden at the thought
of what he had written over the course of his life? Could the
man who created the outspoken Wife of Bath – and who wrote
probably the most famous fart joke in all of English literature
– really have sought to erase such work from his legacy?

What makes these questions particularly complicated for
present-day readers is the image of Chaucer that has accumu-
lated over the last six centuries: that of a brilliant poet who was
playful, ironic, self-deprecating and – perhaps above all, in the
contemporary imagination – amusing. Which precise quality
comes to be in ascendance has shifted over time, with these and
other characteristics periodically coming to the fore in Chaucer
commentary and then receding into the background. The fifteenth century celebrated him as the first master of poetic
eloquence in English. To this picture the sixteenth century
added praise of his social satire and his apparent anticipation of
Reformation values. By the eighteenth century, while some writers might have described the 'Temper' of the so-called Father of
English Poetry as 'a mixture of the gay, the modest, and the
grave', Daniel Defoe declared Chaucer's bawdy texts 'not fit for
Modest persons to read'.[6] Such objections notwithstanding, the
next century saw a new surge of scholarly interest in Chaucer's
life and works, as well as the publication of the first children's

adaptations of Chaucer in 1833. By the end of the twentieth century, Chaucer's name had become synonymous with ribaldry.[7] More recently, some of Chaucer's work has increasingly come under scrutiny for its latent misogyny, antisemitism or racism, a shift that has prompted readers to reflect more deeply on the ethics of the entertainment Chaucer's works so often provide.

This book considers Chaucer's life and work in relation to his reputation for mirth and merriment, in order to explore how he became the poet he is for us today. Not all of Chaucer's readers have considered him to be first and foremost a writer of comic verse, but this does not mean that a Chaucer biography must ignore his contemporary reputation as a humourist. In fact, when we consider his life through the lens of that reputation, we can see more clearly how a combination of skill, diplomacy and good fortune enabled Chaucer to navigate one of the most turbulent periods of medieval English history.

Chaucer versus 'Chaucer'

One of the greatest complications attached to the task of evaluating Chaucer's life and work is that of assessing what connections – if any – might be drawn between the two. This is further complicated by Chaucer's various narrative voices and personae, which include such figures as the fallible narrator of *Troilus and Criseyde*, the bewildered narrators of his dream poems and his pilgrim avatar in *The Canterbury Tales*. Each of these personae seems like a tantalizing glimpse of what Chaucer *might* have been like, though they have also led some readers to try to prise Chaucer's personae apart from the 'real' or 'historical' Chaucer. At the same time, however, both the historical Chaucer and his various fictionalized portrayals of himself 'have some characteristics in common'.[8] It has even been suggested that perhaps there is no problem to be solved in the first place:

it is not simple-minded to talk of Chaucer as the 'I' of the
poem . . . the roles that can be played by the 'performing
self' are infinite, and one role may merge into another
in a word or a phrase, as in life in a wink or a gesture . . .
Chaucer is simply very much better at it than anyone else.
He is not someone else manipulating the 'I' for rationally
explicable strategic purposes; he *is* the dreamer, as much
and as fully as he *is* Chaucer.[9]

How, then, should we read Chaucer's self-deprecating narrators in relation to his life? His narrator avatar 'Geffrey' in the
poem *The House of Fame* hangs petrified in the claws of the eagle
carrying him through the heavens and complaining about how
heavy he is. Might Chaucer be poking fun at himself here? In
the Prologue to the *Legend of Good Women*, the dreamer grovels
while he is chastised by the God of Love for having slandered
women with his poetry (all of which was, of course, written by
Chaucer himself). Is Chaucer making light of actual accusations
levelled against him by audiences or readers? And Chaucer's
pilgrim avatar in *The Canterbury Tales* repeatedly apologizes to
readers for the bawdy tales he is compelled to repeat, lest by
leaving them out he should 'falsen som of my mateere' ('falsify
some of my material', *The Miller's Prologue* 3175). But are any
of these apologies genuine? This is the poet who claims to be a
friend to women, but whose works are filled with misogynistic
stereotypes concerning what women are like and what they
want. While these manoeuvres are often a source of great
amusement to his readers, they also make Chaucer's 'real' voice
and opinions impossible to pin down.

Despite this penchant for self-deprecation and evasiveness,
Chaucer did not shy away from opportunities for self-promotion.
In fact, self-deprecation and self-marketing seem to go hand in
hand in his works. The same passages in which Chaucer is

chastised by the God of Love in the *Legend of Good Women*
include a fairly comprehensive list of the poet's works – love
them or hate them, there they are. In *The Canterbury Tales*, the
Man of Law enumerates the various works written by 'Chaucer,
thogh he kan but lewedly/ On metres and on ryming craftily'
('Chaucer, though he is ignorant/ Of meter and of rhyming
skilfully', *Introduction to the Man of Law's Tale* 47–8), a sly and
ostensibly humble means of providing readers with a list of other
Chaucerian works they might enjoy. Even the very 'Retractions'
that supposedly reject the majority of his works – while piously
approving his translation of Boethius and 'othere bookes of
legendes of seintes, and omelies and moralitee, and devocioun'
('other books of saints' legends, and homilies and morality, and
devotion') – might, from another angle, resemble a catalogue
of his racier texts, a helpful guide for those eager to seek out
what else Chaucer has written, and to select what they would
prefer to read from that body of work. Whether or not Chaucer
was actually stricken with repentance for his 'leccherous' poetry
on his deathbed, and however unlikely it is that Gascoigne's
account, related above, has any basis in historical fact, when
viewed alongside his other apologies and disclaimers, Chaucer's
'Retractions' read as a form of legacy-making-in-advance.

Chaucer's Life

Geoffrey Chaucer was born sometime around 1342. The son of
a prosperous wine merchant, he eventually rose to become a
retainer within some of the grandest households in the country.
The earliest record in which Chaucer is named dates to 1357,
and places him in the household of Elizabeth de Burgh, Countess
of Ulster and wife of Prince Lionel (a son of Edward III). From
there, Chaucer would go on to enjoy a nearly lifelong association
with the fabulously wealthy John of Gaunt, Duke of Lancaster,

who was both the uncle of Richard II and the father of the man who would eventually supplant Richard on the English throne. These connections and Chaucer's travels on the Continent brought him into contact with poets, aristocrats and merchants from all over medieval Europe.

The circumstances of Chaucer's life are important reminders that, while he is best known to us as a poet, he was neither born into a literary household nor specifically employed as a poet during his lifetime. Indeed, though his entry in the *Oxford Dictionary of National Biography* opens by describing Chaucer as a 'poet and administrator', these descriptors might easily be reversed to more accurately reflect his curriculum vitae. In addition to his household positions, Chaucer was at various points in his career a diplomat, a customs officer in the port of London, a Justice of the Peace in Kent, clerk of the king's works and a deputy forester in Somerset. At the same time, of course, Chaucer's poetic work both derived from and increased his access to social circles with a vested interest in promoting, patronizing and enjoying literature in English. Late fourteenth-century England was undergoing its own sort of culture wars, which in turn were closely connected to the very real ongoing war with France now known as the Hundred Years' War.[10] And despite having long had a rich insular literary tradition, England's cultural impact did not yet extend far beyond its shores. Chaucer's writings were among the first poems in English to rival the literature of continental Europe in the eyes of his contemporaries.

If one looks more closely at both Chaucer's life and his writing, it is remarkable to note how little either seems to have been deeply affected by the turmoil that marked the end of the fourteenth century. Chaucer had the fortune (or misfortune) of living in interesting times. The social, religious and political upheaval of fourteenth-century England and Europe may have created opportunities for some ambitious men and women, but it could also put them in jeopardy. The bureaucrat and writer Thomas Usk, for example, was 'impeached of treason in full parliament and condemned to be drawn and hanged'; the *Westminster Chronicle* records that he was 'hanged and immediately taken down and, after about thirty strokes of the axe, beheaded'.[11] The ravages of the plague (which first arrived on England's shores in the summer of 1348) destabilized the social structure of medieval England, setting the stage for the social conflicts that would eventually culminate in the Peasants' Revolt of 1381. The 1380s and '90s were marked by multiple clashes between Richard II and Parliament, as the former sought to rule with absolute authority and the latter sought to limit the king's power. Anxiety concerning the rise of various heretical sects was also beginning to take hold. Chaucer lived long enough to bear witness to all of this and, at the end of his life, saw one dynasty replaced by another when Henry Bolingbroke deposed Richard in 1399 and took his place on the English throne. And yet Chaucer emerged from each episode of turbulence relatively unscathed: he 'kept a low profile in the political conflicts of his day, steering clear of potential trouble in his public life and never mentioning anything controversial in his poetry', strategies that may have been aided by the kind of non-committal good humour, self-deprecation and irony one encounters in his work.[12]

Spaces and Places

If Chaucer's life and writing were not drastically influenced by the events of his time, they were certainly closely bound up with the spaces in which he moved and the places where he lived and laboured. London was where he began his life and where he would later return to work, and his writings make the bustle, clamour and character of that city and its environs come alive. In *The Canterbury Tales*, the 'Cook of Londoun' describes the public spaces of the eastern part of the city as filled with noise and activity, whether it be a 'ridyng' ('procession'; *The Cook's Tale* 4377) in Cheapside or raucous music accompanying a prisoner being led to Newgate Prison (the site on which the Old Bailey now stands; *The Cook's Tale* 4402). The Canterbury pilgrims begin their journey at an inn in Southwark on the south side of the Thames, a 'hostelrye' able to accommodate dozens of people from various backgrounds who were preparing to embark on their journeys.

Chaucer's work also took him to numerous destinations around England, though little documentation survives related to his specific roles and experiences during those domestic travels. As a youth in the service of the Countess of Ulster, he would have accompanied the household on trips to royal residences, some of which were as far-flung as Bristol or Liverpool.[13] His later position as Clerk of the King's Works (in charge of overseeing various building projects on the king's behalf) would have taken him to 'Westminster, the Tower of London, St George's Chapel at Windsor and other royal castles, lodges, and manors'.[14]

Chaucer's travels also frequently took him beyond the borders of his own country and brought him into contact with languages and cultures whose influence can still be perceived in his writing. Documents surviving from Chaucer's lifetime indicate that he undertook at least fourteen trips abroad between 1359 and 1387, though there may well have been more.[15] Most of these journeys took him to France or to Flanders. Other Continental destinations included Florence, Genoa and Navarre (in northern Spain).[16] And of course, the world also came to Chaucer: both his royal connections and his years living and working in London meant that he would have been in contact with travellers and immigrants from around the world.

In addition to visiting a wide variety of places in England and continental Europe, Chaucer also inhabited many different kinds of spaces during his lifetime. As the son of a wine merchant and as a customs officer in London later in his life, he would have moved through warehouses, docks and markets – we can glimpse traces of these environments in his depictions of tradesmen and merchants in *The Canterbury Tales*. As a member of a noble household and as a diplomat, he visited palaces and great houses in England and on the Continent, experiences that may have inspired some of the descriptions of glamorous courts and beautiful gardens found in his poetry. But at the end of his life, he would return one last time to London and its environs, ensconced in a tenement in the garden of the Lady Chapel of Westminster Abbey.[17]

If the places and spaces that Chaucer inhabited shaped his writing, his literary legacy helped determine what kinds of places

Tomb of Geoffrey Chaucer, Poets' Corner, Westminster Abbey.

and spaces would be forever linked with his name. The places associated with Chaucer's remains and those of his descendants are further indicators of the status he had achieved by the end of his life, and the connections he had been able to forge on behalf of his family. Chaucer is buried in the south transept of Westminster Abbey, a space now known as 'Poets' Corner'. His son, Thomas Chaucer (d. 1434), is buried in a magnificent tomb with his wife, Matilda (or Maud), not far from the elaborate transi tomb of their daughter, Alice de la Pole, Duchess of Suffolk, in St Mary the Virgin Church at Ewelme in Oxfordshire. Both Chaucer's cultural significance and the elevated social status of his descendants prompted a number of early biographers and editors to lay particular emphasis on his family's ties to royalty and nobility; for example, the engraving by John Speed of Chaucer and his family tree (included in Thomas Speght's 1598 edition of Chaucer's collected works) displays his connections to England's royal family via his wife's sister, Katherine Swynford,

Tomb of Alice de la Pole, St Mary the Virgin Church, Ewelme.

John Speed's engraving from Thomas Speght's edition of Chaucer's *Workes* (1598), including Chaucer's family tree.

who had married John of Gaunt. This rather distant branch of Chaucer's family tree extends along the left-hand side of a large portrait of Chaucer himself, which is also framed by a reference to his probable father-in-law, 'Payne Roet *Knight*', and by a branch on the right-hand side terminating in Edmund de la Pole, Duke of Suffolk.[18] This family tree is one of many examples of how post-medieval editors and artists eagerly insinuated as much ennoblement as they could into Chaucer's biography.

Marginal miniature of Chaucer, from a manuscript of Thomas Hoccleve's *The Regiment of Princes*, 1425–50.

'fadir reverent'

Practically from the moment of his death in 1400, Chaucer was viewed as a father figure by English poets. Writing sometime in the first decade of the fifteenth century, the poet Thomas Hoccleve (1368–1426), for example, referred to Chaucer as 'fadir reverent', or 'reverent father', in his *Regiment of Princes*.[19] Given Chaucer's historical importance, and his status in English literary history today, it is sometimes difficult to remember that writing poetry was something he did in his spare time, rather than his day job. In his incomplete dream poem *The House of Fame*, Chaucer paints a rather underwhelming picture of what such a life might have looked like in the late fourteenth century. The life of the dreamer-poet 'Geffrey' (apparently a figure for Chaucer himself) appears to be one of dull routine: according to his eagle guide, instead of either resting or seeking out great tidings – or even news of his neighbours – as source material for his poetry, Geffrey comes directly home from work after he has finished his 'rekenynges' (accounts) and sits down to read a book until he is positively dizzy. One can visualize such a poet dragging himself home from his office job and squeezing what little reading and writing time he can out of the remainder of his waking hours. Instead of introspection or divine inspiration, *The House of Fame* paints a picture of a life in which the writing of poetry takes place in circumstances marked by isolation, exhaustion and boredom. Thankfully, the dreamer's life eventually gets more interesting: the eagle transports him to a gleaming palace where he can witness the goddess Fame distributing both good reputations and infamy to the deserving and undeserving alike. Compared with what the eagle says the dreamer usually does, this spectacle is certainly a change of pace.

If the picture painted by *The House of Fame* reflects anything of Chaucer's lived experience as a poet, it is even more remarkable that such a dazed and dogged figure should someday be labelled the father of English poetry. Instead of following in the footsteps of classical and medieval poets who proclaimed themselves to be inspired by the gods, the Muses or Nature, Chaucer depicts himself arriving at the work for which he is now most famous after a long day of number-crunching, only capable of finding inspiration in the words of others rather than in his own genius or via some divine gift. Chaucer's ability to paint this kind of self-deprecating portrait so deftly makes it easy to forget that he did not write poetry for a living, or perhaps even for patronage.[20]

'our faire langage'

Though Chaucer may well have written poems in French (the dominant literary language in England at the time), it was for his works in English that he would come to be known. In the very act of writing poetry in English, Chaucer was doing something artistically ambitious. While it was not uncommon to translate poetry from other languages into English (Chaucer himself did so), few people composed prestigious or high-status poetry in English, at least not at the time when Chaucer began to write:

> Before the 15th century, the overwhelming majority
> of books in England (among the small elite who owned
> them) were in Latin and French. Being taught to read
> and write in England meant being taught to read and
> write Latin, not English. French came second to Latin
> in importance and prestige . . . English was widely used
> but little valued.[21]

Viewing Chaucer's choice to write ambitious poetry in English in this context reveals how creatively daring and unusual it was, and hints at one reason for his fame among his contemporaries and imitators.

Thomas Hoccleve was not the only early fifteenth-century poet to take inspiration from Chaucer's work. In the eyes of the monk John Lydgate (c. 1370–c. 1451), Chaucer was the epitome of poetic achievement in English, the 'Floure of poetes thorghout al Breteyne [flower of poets throughout all Britain]', and Lydgate made countless references and allusions to him and his work in his own verse.[22] Like Hoccleve's description of Chaucer as 'fadir reverent', these early homages to Chaucer singled him out among English writers for his elevation of the

English language. Lydgate's allusions to Chaucer's verse often go even further, offering a miniature catalogue of Chaucer's many writings or a snapshot of their generic variety.

The high esteem in which Chaucer's works were held by later medieval writers is one indication of his importance in the years following his death. Another is the early publication history of Chaucerian texts. While no copies of Chaucer's writings can be dated to his lifetime or identified as having been written in his hand, high-quality copies of his works, such as the Ellesmere manuscript of *The Canterbury Tales* (now held in the Huntington Library in San Marino, California), were produced within the earliest decades of the fifteenth century. More than eighty fifteenth-century manuscripts and fragments of *The Canterbury Tales* survive, of which at least fifty are complete or mostly complete. Copies of texts such as *Troilus and Criseyde*, *The Parliament of Fowls* and *The Legend of Good Women* may be found in dozens of other medieval manuscripts. Some are luxurious productions, commissioned by the wealthy and powerful. Others are simpler copies assembled by professional scribes or scribal teams to be sold at a more modest price. And some appear to have been copied by individuals for their own purposes.

In the years following Chaucer's death, increases in literacy and in manuscript production enabled more readers to own or access the works of English authors than at any other point in medieval history. Men and women from a variety of backgrounds owned and read manuscripts of Chaucer's works, occasionally inscribing their names or family mottos in the margins and fly-leaves of their copies. And though the earliest collection of Chaucer's works would not be produced until the middle of the sixteenth century, one fifteenth-century manuscript now in the Cambridge University Library is an early attempt at such a collection: it includes *The Canterbury Tales*, *Troilus and Criseyde* and some of Chaucer's dream poems.[23]

The arrival of print on England's shores in the later fifteenth century made it possible to produce highly uniform copies of Chaucer's works more quickly than ever before. The man who brought the printing press to England, William Caxton (c. 1422– c. 1491), would print several of Chaucer's works, including *Troilus and Criseyde*, *The House of Fame*, *The Parliament of Fowls* and two editions of *The Canterbury Tales*, as well as Chaucer's prose translation of Boethius' *Consolation of Philosophy*. Caxton clearly felt there was a thriving market for print copies of Chaucer, who (as he put it) 'for his ornate wrytyng in our tongue maye wel have the name of a laureate poete'.[24] And while manuscripts and luxury copies of printed books would continue to be produced into the sixteenth century, over time print ensured that Chaucer's works became increasingly affordable and accessible.

When one considers developments in fifteenth-century book production alongside Chaucer's decision to write his poetry in English, it is easy to see how Chaucer loomed over the final century of medieval English poetry. He produced a body of work distinguished by its remarkable breadth and variety. *The Canterbury Tales* alone contains a wide range of genres and forms, from the didactic prose of the *Tale of Melibee* to the beast fable, short comic texts, classical narratives, saint's lives and other genres among the other tales. His translations of such texts as the French *Roman de la rose* earned the praise of his contemporaries (the French poet Eustache Deschamps dubbed him 'Grant translateur', or 'great translator').[25] He did not shy away from Italian source material either: *Troilus and Criseyde*, his magnificent reworking of Giovanni Boccaccio's (1313–1375) tale of a doomed love affair during the Trojan War, is his only complete longer work. His shorter poems include satirical, didactic and comic verse, as well as love lyrics. And readers continue to be charmed by his dream poems and intrigued by his prose *Treatise on the Astrolabe*. Regardless of the fact that a number of

his better-known poems survive in only incomplete or fragmen-
tary form, Chaucer continues to dominate our picture of later
medieval English literature.

'Myrthe'

Given the variety of works he wrote, how did Chaucer come to be
so closely associated with comic writing, merriment and humour?

He may not have set out to be known as a merry poet, but
Chaucer's texts suggest that he did, at the very least, think it was
important to amuse his readers. Near the end of the *General
Prologue* to *The Canterbury Tales*, when the pilgrims agree to take
part in a tale-telling competition, the innkeeper or 'Host' Harry
Bailly, who presides over the competition, explains that to win,
the tale must be not only edifying but entertaining:

> And which of yow that bereth hym best of alle –
> That is to seyn, that telleth in this caas
> Tales of best sentence and moost solaas –
> Shal have a soper at oure aller cost[.]

> And whichever of you that does best of all –
> That is to say, that tells in this instance
> Tales of best moral meaning and most pleasure –
> Shall have a supper at the cost of us all.
> (796–9)

That Chaucer's *oeuvre* managed to strike a balance between
'sentence' and 'solaas' is suggested by the remarks of the very first
person to publish his works in print. In the prologue he composed for his second edition of *The Canterbury Tales* (printed
circa 1483), Caxton described the variety of its contents, among
which could be found tales 'of noblesse/ wysedom/ gentyllesse/

Myrthe/ and also of veray holynesse and vertue [of nobleness, wisdom, gentleness, mirth and also of true holiness and virtue]'.[26] The word *myrthe* or *mirthe* – which stands out somewhat in such a serious list – had a variety of meanings in Middle English (the collection of English dialects spoken between the Norman Conquest and the end of the fifteenth century). Like its modern English equivalent, Middle English *mirthe* could refer to joy or happiness, as well as merriment, but it also carried additional meanings: it could refer to a source of entertainment or amusement, and could even serve as a euphemism for lovemaking. Chaucer himself uses *mirthe* in both these latter senses, and occasionally seems to play upon the word's ambiguity. When the young clerk Nicholas and Alison the carpenter's wife are cavorting in *The Miller's Tale*, Chaucer tells us that they spent the night 'In bisynesse of myrthe and of solas [in the business of sexual delight and pleasure]' (3654), and yet he uses the same word pairing in the ill-fated *Tale of Sir Thopas* when his pilgrim avatar describes the tale he is about to tell as one 'Of myrthe and of solas [of amusement and pleasure]' (714). Over the centuries, Chaucer's name would gradually become synonymous with the rather more obscene form of mirth that features in *The Canterbury Tales*, so much so that a 1993 essay on the use of authors' names as adjectives defined 'Chaucerian' as 'bawdy in an acceptably Olde Englisshe way' (though the acceptability of this side of Chaucer's humour has increasingly been called into question).[27]

Caxton did not pluck his words out of thin air. In fact, he very likely derived them directly from Lydgate. In the Prologue to a poem called *The Siege of Thebes*, which Lydgate pretends to narrate as one of Chaucer's pilgrim characters en route to Canterbury, Lydgate explains that, among *The Canterbury Tales*, readers will find

Some of desport, some of moralité,
Some of knyghthode, love, and gentillesse,
And some also of parfit holynesse,
And some also in soth of ribaudye
To make laughter in the companye.

Some of merry-making, some of morality
Some about knighthood, love, and nobility,
And some also of perfect holiness,
And some also, in truth, of ribaldry
To create laughter in the group.   (22–6)

While Caxton's list of descriptors echoes the list above, Lydgate's description of *The Canterbury Tales* places notably greater emphasis on the collection's entertainment value, and in particular on the ability of some tales to provoke laughter. Perhaps most strikingly, Lydgate concludes his list with a reference to Chaucer's *ribaudye* – the bawdy escapades and fart jokes that have remained famous to this day.

The shift from Lydgate's emphasis on the entertainment value of Chaucer's work to Caxton's emphasis on its morality is an excellent example-in-miniature of how the reception of Chaucer's works has varied from his death in 1400 to the present day. Mirth has, however, remained one of his most persistent trademarks. *The Canterbury Tales* is most closely associated with this side of Chaucer, of course, given its various experimentations with the *fabliau* genre (short comic tales featuring illicit sex and trickery). Within 25 years of Chaucer's death, inventive scribes were imitating his bawdy *fabliau* style in spurious expansions of his depictions of illicit sex, adding more than a dozen lines of graphic detail to the famous sex scene in a pear tree that marks the beginning of the end of *The Merchant's Tale*. (These spurious lines would later be expelled from Chaucer's text in 1775 by Thomas

Tyrwhitt, who described them as 'superfluous ribaldry'.[28]) Around the same time that these textual interventions were made in manuscripts of *The Canterbury Tales*, Lydgate was completing work on *The Siege of Thebes* (c. 1421–2), whose prologue has an oddly medicalized fart joke that reads like an homage to Chaucer's occasionally scatological humour. Such adaptations and spin-off narratives featuring Chaucerian ribaldry have been produced from the middle of the fifteenth century up to the present day.

If Chaucer's other works have not attracted as much attention for their humour over the years, both dark- and light-hearted comedy are nonetheless there to be found. In *Troilus and Criseyde*, we find the figure of Pandarus, the dodgy uncle who pushes his niece Criseyde into a sexual relationship with the Trojan prince Troilus, in part by means of ribald jokes. (Pandarus would eventually – partly by way of Shakespeare – lend his name to the word 'pander', a go-between or pimp.) The chirping and squawking of the avian debate in *The Parliament of Fowls* is an amusing parody of human parliamentary procedure and its accompanying squabbles. And in shorter poems like Chaucer's *envoys* (letters) to two of his acquaintances ('Bukton' and 'Scogan'), we see his sense of humour at work in a more intimate context, teasing members of a coterie audience.

By the sixteenth century, Chaucer's humour and even his ribaldry were linked to his reputation as a social satirist. His skewering of corrupt friars and other members of the clergy struck a chord with those readers of Reformation England who were in the process of severing ties with the Roman Church. Sixteenth-century writers lauded Chaucer for shining a light on the vices of his age – to them he was something of a proto-Protestant who rightly drew attention to the venality of the Church and its clergy. But by the seventeenth century, this 'moral Chaucer' had become 'merry Chaucer': a jolly, antiquated figure whose works might no longer be read in their original Middle English by many, but who was nonetheless known as an author of entertaining and occasionally ribald material. This led to lively adaptations of his *fabliaux* in the eighteenth century (as well as the censorship of Chaucer's bawdy texts by that century's conclusion).

As medieval English literature became an object of serious study in the nineteenth century, the image of 'merry Chaucer', man of *mirthe*, came to the fore. Frederick J. Furnivall, one of the nineteenth century's most enthusiastic promoters of the study of medieval English literature and the founder of both the Early English Text Society and the Chaucer Society, described Chaucer as 'the most genial and humourful healthy-souled man that England had ever seen'.[29] Statements like this may be found throughout the Chaucer scholarship produced since Furnivall's lifetime, and have fostered a 'desire to like Chaucer, to idealize him, to believe in a Chaucer who laughs "with, not at human weakness"'.[30] But one could argue that this desire has shaped opinion of the medieval poet for longer centuries. Thus, while *mirthe* is not the only lens through which we might consider Chaucer's life and legacy (or even, some might argue, the most important), it is a lens that enables us to consider one of the most enduring aspects of his literary legacy, and one that over time has become increasingly intertwined with his biography.

* * *

This book aims to tell the story of Chaucer's life and career in a way that sheds light on what has become one of the most distinctive aspects of his fame: his reputation as a 'merry' author whose works entertain and provoke laughter, not infrequently by means of bawdy humour. This aspect of his writing originated in Chaucer's sense of the world in which he lived and his sense of his own place within that world. His self-deprecation emerges out of his acute awareness of the status of English literature as the cultural upstart of his day. His satire responds to the anxieties and troubles of later medieval England and Europe, even as it often slides away from direct critique. Chaucer had an eye for both hypocrisy and incongruity on the one hand and unlikely consistencies on the other, consistencies that sometimes spanned social, political or religious boundaries. His abilities as an observer served him well in his writing, as they may have served him in his ever-evolving professional career.

Though the overall trajectory of this book is roughly chronological, its aim is to orientate developments in Chaucer's experimentations with humorous modes of writing in relation to key episodes in his life and times. Each chapter is focused on a particular theme that unites these two focal points of the book. Throughout, this book is concerned with a variety of questions: how does Chaucer make fun and poke fun? How does Chaucer make us laugh? Why does Chaucer try to make us laugh? Why is this such a distinctive aspect of his contemporary reputation? Where did that come from? How might it be connected to the events and circumstances of his life? What do we see more clearly (and less clearly) when we focus on his *mirthe*?

As we will see, Chaucer used humour for many different purposes throughout his literary career, not the least of which was forging that career. And yet Chaucer was not what we might call a professional poet, nor did he ever refer to himself as a 'poet' of any sort in his writings. 'Maker' or 'compilator' (compiler), perhaps, but never 'poet' or 'author', terms that were, if possible, even more loaded in the Middle Ages than they are now. But by looking at those areas of his life in which Chaucer was *not* a poet, we can gain a clearer sense of how he became the poet he is for us today.

TWO

Connections

If you walk along Upper Thames Street between Blackfriars Bridge and London Bridge today, it is hard to imagine how that part of London looked and sounded in the late four-teenth century. The sound of traffic drowns out the river only a few minutes' walk away. The shiny modern buildings of the City of London loom on every side. But some clues regarding the street's medieval past are still visible, clues such as a small side passage labelled 'Vintners' Court', which leads off in the direction of the Thames.

It was near here, in what is still known as Vintry Ward, that Geoffrey Chaucer likely spent the first years of his life. The ward takes its name from the many wine merchants whose premises and homes filled the area in the Middle Ages, and it is still the home of the Worshipful Company of Vintners, whose first Royal Charter dates to 1363 (though the company's roots may be older).[1] Such 'guilds' or associations of merchants and crafts-people connected to specific trades sprang up all over England in the later Middle Ages. They protected their members' economic interests and often wielded considerable power.

Chaucer was born into this mercantile world sometime in the early 1340s. His father, John Chaucer (c. 1312–1366), was a prosperous London vintner.[2] Less is known of Geoffrey's mother, Agnes Chaucer, née Copton (d. 1381); she is mentioned in doc-uments as early as October 1349 as the wife of John Chaucer, after whose death in 1366 she married Bartholomew Chappel, another vintner.[3] In his youth, John had taken part in a number of military campaigns, including the uprising of Henry, Earl of Lancaster, against Queen Isabella and Roger Mortimer, for which John was outlawed in 1329.[4] But within a few years of Geoffrey's birth, John was appointed deputy king's butler and owned 'an impressive catalogue of land and properties for someone outside the nobility'.[5] The Chaucer family's prosperity and connections gave Geoffrey a good start in life, securing him positions within noble and royal households.

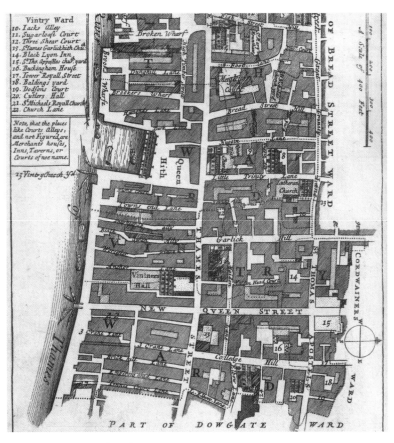

Vintry Ward, 17th century.

Almost nothing is known of Geoffrey's childhood, including whether or not he had siblings.[6] While it is unclear whether Geoffrey was born in Vintry Ward, his father certainly had a house there, in which Geoffrey probably spent his earliest years and which remained in the family until 19 June 1381, when Geoffrey transferred its deed to one Henry Herbury.[7] The property is described as having 'houses built above, solars [private rooms located in the upper floors], cellars, and other appurtenances', a comfortable home typical of a well-to-do mercantile family.[8] Some sense of what such a house might have looked like may be gained from the Medieval Merchant's House in Southampton (originally built sometime around 1290), which also belonged to a prosperous wine merchant: the original structure included cellar space for storage of goods, a shop space at the front and living spaces for the family.[9] The merchants living in London's Vintry Ward in the late fourteenth century would have likewise both lived in and worked out of such buildings, whose overhanging upper stories often jutted out over the street to maximize their floor space. The Chaucer house extended 'in length from the royal street of Thames Street on the south up to the water of the Walbrook on the north'.[10] The Walbrook carried sewage and other waste away from the house before emptying it into the Thames, which may have had unpleasant consequences when the stream overflowed at times when the tidewaters were exceptionally high (perhaps this is one reason why it was vaulted over in the first half of the fifteenth century).[11]

An area in which living spaces and mercantile spaces jostled together, the fourteenth-century Vintry Ward would have been filled with the competing sounds of domestic life and commerce. Nobles and wealthy citizens lived alongside members of the mercantile class, and Englishmen rubbed shoulders with merchants, traders and families from other countries, including Gascon and

Medieval Merchant's House, Southampton.

Italian traders resident in the area as well as visitors passing
through on business. The area was also home to Flemish traders
and families from Flanders and other parts of the Low Countries.
On any given day, the streets of Vintry Ward would have rung
with voices speaking in a variety of languages. But while people
from different social backgrounds and nationalities lived side
by side there, this cohabitation was not always peaceful. The
Anonimalle Chronicle records that during the 1381 Peasants'
Revolt dozens of Flemings were dragged from the local parish
church of St Martin Vintry on Friday, 14 June, and beheaded,

their bodies left piled up on the street.[12] The Chaucer house was located in the parish of St Martin Vintry, and was in fact on the same street.[13] One can well imagine that, when Geoffrey transferred the deed to the house five days after this gruesome incident, the transaction may have been accompanied by some sense of relief.

Although the Chaucer house was in the parish of St Martin Vintry (the church most closely associated with the wine merchants of the area), there were several other churches nearby, and no evidence survives indicating to which of these churches Chaucer may have belonged. Likewise, though there were schools in the area at which Chaucer might have studied as a child (including one at St Paul's Cathedral), no evidence has been uncovered that he did so. Given his family's position, it is more likely that he attended some sort of school than that he was privately educated at home.[14] In the schoolroom, Chaucer would have begun the study of Latin, grammar, composition, translation and debate.[15] But he would soon have the opportunity to acquire a very different sort of education in a much more rarefied atmosphere.

Moving Up in the World

In the 1357 accounts of the household expenditures of Elizabeth, Countess of Ulster, is a note explaining that one 'Galfrido Chaucer' had been given, among other things, gifts of clothing appropriate to a relatively low-ranking member of the household. These gifts included a 'paltok' (short tunic or doublet) of the sort that a page might wear.[16] In great medieval households, attendants were frequently given such items in return for their services, particularly in preparation for important events or feast days; in the same year, for example, Elizabeth is recorded as having given Chaucer 2s 6d 'for necessaries for the feast of the Nativity'.[17]

By 1357, Chaucer would have been in his adolescence. In later medieval England, infancy lasted from birth until the age of seven, childhood until the age of fourteen. Adolescence was the stage of a young person's life at which he or she might be sent away from home to serve in other households. This experience would, it was hoped, 'train and discipline' young people and 'give them patrons who could assist their careers, and relieve their parents of expense'.[18] Serving in a noble or royal household would have been an excellent start in life for any young person in late fourteenth-century England, and the fact that John Chaucer had at one time been deputy butler to the king may have helped him to secure this opportunity for his son, Geoffrey.

It is unclear when and in precisely what capacity Chaucer served the Countess of Ulster, though he may well have served as a page. Boys could serve as pages between the ages of seven and fourteen, during which time they would be responsible for carrying out a variety of tasks, such as caring for their lord's clothing, delivering messages and serving at meals. In the process, they would learn about courtly manners, the basics of combat and the running of an important household. Whereas the modern household is largely centred on the location of one's accommodation, in the later Middle Ages it was centred on 'a person rather than around a particular building or place'; thus, a lord or lady's household would include not only themselves and their family but 'their dependents; their extensive retinue or household officers, servants, and hangers-on; their horses and other animals, and a vast quantity of furnishings and furniture, all of which piled into carriages and carts and then unloaded into manor houses littered around the country'.[19] Since the household in which Chaucer was working was connected to the royal family, it would have moved around a great deal, visiting the greatest and most refined homes in the land. While mingling with, learning from and being cared for by some of the most powerful people in England,

Chaucer also would have had the chance to mingle with boys and girls his own age who were serving in similar positions. The 1357 household records in which Chaucer's name is first recorded also note the gift of a tunic to one 'Philippe Pan' (that is, Philippa Pan), possibly the same Philippa who was a daughter of Sir Gilles de Roet (known as Paon) and, later, Chaucer's wife.[20]

The education young Geoffrey received during his time in the service of the Countess of Ulster would have covered more than just the social graces necessary to secure a profitable position in the world. While he did not necessarily have a close relationship with his mistress and her family, his position would have given him the opportunity to learn from the tastemakers of later medieval Europe, the men and women who shaped the cultural fashions of their time, encompassing everything from clothing and manners to music, art and literature. It is very likely that he was among the participants in lavish banquets and major events connected to the life of the royal family. This may have included 'preparations for the betrothal of the countess's infant daughter to Edmund Mortimer, earl of March', or even 'the funeral of the dowager queen Isabella' in 1358.[21] On such occasions, encounters with members of other aristocratic households and visitors from the Continent would have given him a sense not only of his household's place in the pecking order of fourteenth-century English society, but of England's place in the world. He would have witnessed all of this from the perspective of a member of the mercantile class attempting to adapt to the aristocratic environment around him and eager to learn what might help him succeed in that rarefied atmosphere.

We can glimpse what that process of adaptation might have entailed in the conduct literature that survives from the later Middle Ages, texts that advised readers regarding what behaviour was appropriate to their station in life. The fifteenth-century Middle English poem *Stans Puer ad Mensam* (The Child at Table), originally derived from a thirteenth-century Latin source, advises young boys to practise 'vertuous disciplyne' when eating before their social superiors: they should look their betters in the eye when speaking to them, refrain from picking their noses, wash their hands before coming to the table and neither speak nor laugh with their mouths full.[22] In the later Middle Ages, one's ability to follow such advice (the same lessons parents attempt to teach young children today) might make the crucial difference between social success and failure. These conduct texts remind us that, while people in Chaucer's position may have been observing their social superiors, they themselves were also under observation; consequently, they must 'ever thinke on worshype and thy onesté,/ And kepe thee ever fro rebuke and all maner repreve [always think about your reputation and your sense of decorum and keep yourself safe from rebuke and all kinds of reproof]'.[23]

An attendant in an aristocratic household would have needed not only good manners but intelligence and tact if he was to ingratiate himself with his master or mistress. Geoffrey must have conducted himself well enough in the service of the Countess of Ulster: by October 1360, he had transferred his services to the household of Lionel, Earl of Ulster. Geoffrey is mentioned in Lionel's household accounts for that year in connection with a journey from Calais to England, on which he may well have accompanied the earl.[24] Later that same year, Geoffrey became an attendant in the greatest English household of all: that of King Edward III himself.

In the King's Service

Surviving documents indicate that Chaucer served as valet and squire in the king's household, where he would have been in a truly glamorous atmosphere.[25] At this point in his reign, Edward

III was at the height of his power and popularity. By now in his late forties, he had conducted relatively successful military campaigns in pursuit of his claim to the French throne, the claim that would launch what would eventually become known as the Hundred Years' War. This long string of armed conflicts, which would preoccupy England and France between 1337 and 1453, had begun less than a decade before Chaucer was born, when Edward first attempted to claim the French throne through his mother Isabella, sister of the late Charles IV of France. Since French law did not permit succession through the female line, Philip, Count of Valois and Charles's patrilineal cousin, ascended to the throne, setting off an international conflict that would continue intermittently for more than a century.

Serving as a royal attendant during such a conflict was not without risks. While taking part in Edward's 1359 military campaigns in France (most probably as a member of Lionel's household), Geoffrey was captured and held for ransom.[26] His ransom was paid from the king's accounts; William de Farley, then Keeper of the King's Wardrobe, notes a payment of £16 paid for Geoffrey Chaucer after the latter had been 'captured by enemies, in payment for his release'.[27] The payment should not necessarily be taken as an indication of any particular regard that either Edward or Lionel might have had for the young Geoffrey – indeed, it is quite possible that Geoffrey was not known to either man personally. De Farley records ransom payments of as much as £50 (for Richard Stury, the king's squire) and as little as 40s (for Richard Dulle, an archer), which puts Chaucer's ransom payment somewhere in the bottom third of amounts paid. But the incident does give us some sense of how Chaucer personally experienced the great conflict of his time. He may have drawn on these experiences during his composition of *The Knight's Tale*, in which two cousins of royal blood are pulled from beneath a heap of bodies on the battlefield and held by a king who refuses to ransom them. Chaucer's personal experience of these French campaigns would have acquainted him with such grim imagery, and with the ransom culture of later medieval warfare.

The English had won major victories against France in the years prior to Chaucer's move to the royal household, the most notable of which was the Battle of Poitiers in September 1356, when the heir to the English throne, Edward the Black Prince, managed to capture none other than King John II of France himself. To this martial glory was added the carefully cultivated elegance of Edward III's court. The king was deeply invested in promoting chivalric culture within his household and among the aristocracy, whose ranks were swelled by his expansion of the peerage after having stalled somewhat during the reigns of Edward's father and grandfather, Edward II and Edward I. Edward III also attempted to present himself as the contemporary heir to the legacy of the legendary King Arthur, and even planned for some years to revive the fabled Round Table, though these plans were never carried out.[28] Sometime around 1348, however, he formed the Order of the Garter, the idea for which, according to legend, originated in an incident that took place at a ball. When a lady with whom Edward III was dancing dropped her garter, Edward purportedly picked it up and tied it around his own leg. In response to the laughter of those around him, he uttered the words that would become the order's motto: *Honi soit qui mal y pense* (Shame on him who thinks ill of it). While these events may never have taken place, the story is consistent with both Edward's eager revival of the chivalric code and the values reminiscent of Arthurian romance. It is perhaps for this very reason that the order's motto may be found added to the final page of the manuscript of the late fourteenth-century poem *Sir Gawain and the Green Knight*, a text in which the reputation of Arthur's court is at stake.[29]

Chaucer's time in the service of English royalty was a period of eye-opening experiences for the young man. As a participant in the early stages of the war for the French throne, he witnessed bloodshed and destruction on the battlefield, and learned that one's survival could depend on one's connections. As an attendant in the royal retinue, he observed how favours were distributed at court, and how one's success at court depended on one's ability to ingratiate oneself with the wealthy and powerful. As someone whose adolescence and young adulthood were spent in the greatest households of later medieval England, he was exposed to high culture and the pomp and glory on display in these lavish surroundings. These experiences also enabled Chaucer to form one of the most important and enduring connections of his lifetime with one of the most powerful men in fourteenth-century England: John of Gaunt.

John of Gaunt

The third son of Edward III, John of Gaunt (1340–1399) is perhaps most famously depicted in Shakespeare's *Richard II* as a man who feels he is witnessing the end of a glorious era in England's history. In the play, Gaunt lament on his deathbed foreshadows the coming change in England's fortunes, which, unbeknown to him, will be precipitated by his son Henry Bolingbroke's usurpation of Richard II's throne: 'That England that was wont to conquer others/ Hath made a shameful conquest of itself.'[30] Gaunt may not have made a speech about 'this sceptred isle' of England on his actual deathbed, but his life did coincide with what would be an important turning point in England's history.[31]

If Gaunt's son eventually rose to lofty heights, Gaunt himself was also an illustrious man in his own right. He was one of the wealthiest men in late fourteenth-century England, as well as one of the most unpopular. At the beginning of Richard's reign,

Lucas Cornelisz de Kock (attrib.), *John of Gaunt*, 16th century, tempera on panel.

it was feared that he might have designs on the English throne, though no evidence exists to support that idea.[32] His unsuccessful (and costly) attempts to claim the throne of Castile through his second wife, Constance, were viewed as a waste of the nation's resources. In the wake of the Good Parliament of 1376, during which the Commons sought to address what they viewed as the royal mismanagement of the realm (blamed on false advisors and the king's mistress, Alice Perrers), Gaunt's stubborn efforts to reinforce the rights and privileges of the royal family during the Bad Parliament of 1377 made him many enemies among the Commons and the general population. Within a few years, he became a symbol of the alleged corruption that rebels sought to do away with in the 1381 Peasants' Revolt, during the course of which his splendid Savoy Palace was burned to the ground.

It is unclear precisely when and under what circumstances Chaucer and Gaunt first became acquainted. They may have met at Christmas in 1358, when Gaunt was invited to celebrate the holiday with his sister-in-law, Elizabeth of Ulster.[33] Gaunt would have been eighteen years old, and Chaucer a few years younger. They may also have fought in the same division during Edward's 1359 campaign in France, when Chaucer was captured.[34] But within the next decade, the two young men would be linked by a much more personal connection.

In 1366, Chaucer married one Philippa de Roet, possibly the same 'Philippe Pan' mentioned in the 1357 accounting documents that also mention Chaucer. Within a few years (and allegedly after the death of his first wife, Blanche of Lancaster), Gaunt began an affair with Philippa's married sister, Katherine Swynford, whom he also employed as governess to his children. The affair would continue for nearly thirty years until the widowed Katherine became Gaunt's third wife in 1396.

Whatever the nature of the relationship between Gaunt and Chaucer, Katherine's relationship with Gaunt seems to have proven advantageous for both Geoffrey and Philippa over the years. It has even been suggested that a lengthy digression on the subject of governesses in Chaucer's *Physician's Tale* (possibly written before he began *The Canterbury Tales*) may have been his way of teasing his sister-in-law about her love affair with Gaunt. In that passage, Chaucer addresses governesses charged with guarding and educating virtuous 'lordes doghtres' (73), and remarks that they likely got their jobs either because they themselves were virtuous or, conversely, because they themselves had 'falle in freletee ['fallen into frailty'; that is, lost their virtue]' (78), and were therefore familiar with 'the olde daunce' of love and court-ship (79).[35] It is certainly possible that this is a teasing reference to Katherine's relationship with Gaunt. But more obvious traces of Chaucer's connection to Gaunt may be found in a poem writ-ten not long after Chaucer's marriage took place: *The Book of the Duchess*.

The Death of a Duchess

In the summer of 1348, England was plunged into what was per-haps the greatest catastrophe of the European Middle Ages: the 'explosive proliferation' of *Yersinia pestis*, the bacterium that led to the Black Death pandemic.[36] Scholars have very recently established that the European plague outbreak was likely one in a series of outbreaks and bacterial mutations that may have spread westward from the Tian Shan mountains with the thir-teenth-century expansion of the Mongol Empire.[37] Its impact was devastating.

One of the most famous medieval European accounts of the plague's effects appears in the first book of Giovanni Boccaccio's *Decameron*, a work likely completed between 1349 and 1353 and the inspiration for Chaucer's *Canterbury Tales*. Boccaccio describes the desperate attempts of Italian cities to curb the spread of the plague (clearing rubbish out of the city, refusing entry to those who appear ill, appealing to God by means of 'formal processions'), none of which appeared to have had any effect whatsoever. Despite these precautions, the plague spread everywhere. In its earliest stages of infection, those afflicted would develop 'swellings in the groin or the armpit, some of which were egg-shaped whilst others were roughly the size of the common apple'. Bruises would then develop all over the body, an 'infallible' sign of imminent death. 'Against all these maladies, it seemed that all the advice of physicians and all the power of medicine were profitless and unavailing.'[38]

In Europe the plague led to the death of an estimated 25 million people between 1347 and 1352 – more than one-third of the population. In England, over the thirty years that followed the first outbreak in 1348, the Black Death claimed the lives of nearly half the population, wiping out men, women and children from every social background.[39] Neither wealth nor power could ensure one's survival.

On 12 September 1368, Blanche of Lancaster, the wife of John of Gaunt, died at Tutbury Castle in Staffordshire during her husband's absence overseas. While the exact circumstances of her death remain unknown, it is thought that she may have fallen victim to the Black Death, which was rampaging through Europe at the time of her passing. Just 26 years old, she had given her husband seven children, three of whom lived to adulthood and one of whom would eventually become Henry IV of England. Blanche's death seems to have affected Gaunt profoundly; though he would go on to be married twice more, he held annual commemorations of his wife's death until his own 31 years later, when he was buried alongside her in a lavish tomb at St Paul's Cathedral.

Blanche's death proved to be the inspiration for Chaucer's earliest-known major poem in English, and one of the earliest texts in which we see him deploy what would eventually become his distinctive self-deprecation. At the time of Blanche's death, Chaucer was a young man in his twenties. He had spent at least a decade of his life in the service of royalty and was by now well acquainted with the tastes and manners of the English aristocracy, and with the cultural fashions of the court. Within five years of Blanche's death, he used that knowledge to write an elegant poem to commemorate her passing.

The Man in Black

The precise date of *The Book of the Duchess* is difficult to determine. Some have argued that it was written not long after Blanche's death (as early as 1368, but possibly a few years later), though it may have been written for a later annual commemoration. It is quite possible that these commemorations were the result of genuine grief on Gaunt's part – his marriage to Blanche had brought him tremendous wealth, and it seems to have been a happy, or at least companionable, union. As a humble retainer writing in response to a powerful man's deeply personal loss, Chaucer was attempting something that was both ambitious and potentially perilous, should his poetic offering incur the duke's displeasure.

The resulting text is a short dream poem of 1,334 lines. Dream poetry was a highly popular genre of imaginative writing in the Middle Ages, and encompassed a variety of first-person narratives describing the personal experience of a dream or vision. These texts tended to follow a relatively predictable pattern, one that is in evidence in *The Book of the Duchess*: a narrator falls asleep after pondering certain questions, ideas or problems, and then dreams that he finds himself in a different location, not infrequently an idyllic setting such as a lush garden or other outdoor space. Over the course of the poem, the dreamer witnesses certain events and/or encounters characters who lead him on a journey of discovery or revelation, one that often has some connection to whatever topic he was reflecting on at the time he fell asleep. The characters he meets can be historical figures, deities or allegorical personifications, among other possibilities. Upon awakening, the dreamer sometimes declares himself to have found a solution to his original problem, or simply describes himself writing an account of his dreamed experience.

Dream poetry permitted medieval authors to indulge in fantasy, offer carefully veiled critique or frame narratives as the

products of divine revelation. Some of the greatest works of
Middle English literature (including *Piers Plowman* and the anonymous poem now called *Pearl*) take the form of dream poems.
Chaucer himself would compose at least four over the course of
his writing career, in addition to translating the thirteenth-
century French masterpiece *Le Roman de la rose*. In many ways,
it was the perfect genre for a young poet to use in order to commemorate the death of a duchess: it offered opportunities for
learned allusions to other dream poems, enchanting descriptions
of beautiful settings and condolences expressed at a respectful
and socially acceptable remove.

The Book of the Duchess opens with a lament concerning its
narrator's insomnia: 'I have gret wonder, be this lyght,/ How that
I lyve, for day ne nyght/ I may nat slepe wel nygh noght [I feel
great wonder, by this light, that I live, for neither by day nor by
night may I get hardly any sleep at all]' (1–3). The reasons for
this insomnia are unclear, though the narrator's hints that he has
long been suffering from a 'sicknesse' that can only be healed by
one 'phisicien' resemble medieval poetic descriptions of love-
sickness and its symptoms (36–40). Desperate to 'drive the night
away' (49), the narrator reads a book relating the story of King
Ceyx and Queen Alcione, in which the god Morpheus sends the
queen to sleep so that she can receive news of her beloved king's
death in a dream. Upon receiving confirmation that what she
has long feared is in fact true, Queen Alcione dies from sorrow.

At this point in the poem, readers familiar with the circumstances surrounding the poem's composition might anticipate
that Chaucer is about to allude to Blanche's death and Gaunt's
mourning. Instead, he strikes out in a completely different direction. Rather than ponder the tragedy of the tale he has just read,
the poem's narrator realizes, to his own astonishment, that he
has stumbled upon a solution to his insomnia: now that he knows
there is a god 'that koude make/ Men to slepe [that knew how to

make men sleep]' (235–6), he must beg Morpheus to put him to
sleep as well!

At first glance, this reaction seems somewhat incongruous,
given the circumstances surrounding the poem's composition
and the tragic tale that has just been recounted. But it is this
incongruity that makes the diversion *diverting*: solemnity and
grief are displaced by the narrator's astonishment and wonder,
as well as his slightly comical desperation – his ensuing offer to
give Morpheus 'a fether-bed' stuffed with 'down of pure dowves
white [pure white doves' down]' and bedecked in black satin
and gold (250–61) goes on for more than twenty lines. If we
imagine Chaucer reading this poem aloud before an aristocratic
gathering, or at a commemoration of Blanche's death, we can
imagine the accumulation of remembered grief his audience
might have felt as he recounted Alcione's story, and the startling
release that might be afforded by the self-involved narrator's
sudden return to the subject of his own need for sleep.

No sooner has the narrator uttered this promise than his
prayer is answered: he falls asleep and finds himself in a beautiful dreamworld. His chamber is decorated with words and images
from *Le Roman de la rose* and filled with birdsong and the call
of a hunting horn, which draws him outside into a May morning. He follows the distant sound of a hunt in progress until he
encounters a man in black who is the very picture of aristocratic
mourning: 'A wonder wel-farynge knyght . . . clothed al in blak
[a very handsome knight clothed in black]' (452–7), seated
beside a tree with his head hanging low and speaking to himself
'with a dedly sorwful soun [with a deadly, sorrowful sound]'
(462):

> I have of sorwe so gret won
> That joye gete I never non,
> Now that I see my lady bryght,

Which I have loved with al my myght,
Is fro me ded and ys agoon.

I have of sorrow such great abundance
That I never have any joy,
Now that I see my beautiful lady,
Whom I have loved with all my might,
Is dead and gone from me.
(475–9)

Having lost the woman he cared for, the man in black is so dis-
tracted by grief that at first he does not reply when the narrator
stands before him and addresses him. Once he becomes aware of
the narrator and falls into conversation with him, the two men
speak of his loss for more than eight hundred lines. As if he has
not just overheard (and recounted) the knight's very specific
lament, the narrator urges him to disclose the reason for his grief:
'discure me youre woo . . . And telleth me of your sorwes smerte;/
Paraunter hyt may ese youre herte [reveal your woe to me and
tell me of your sorrow's pain; perhaps it may ease your heart]'
(549–56).

The fact that the narrator persistently seems not to know
what has caused the knight's grief (despite having overheard his
explanation) has puzzled some readers. At three points in the
poem, Chaucer's dreamer asks the man in black to explain what
has caused him so much sorrow, to which the knight consistently
replies that 'Thou wost ful lytel what thou menest;/ I have lost
more than thow wenest [You know very little about what you
mean; I have lost more than you realize]' (743–4). The narrator's
actions have been variously interpreted. Some have suggested
that Chaucer intended it to serve as a simple form of comic relief
for his audience, a suggestion likely prompted by the contemporary tendency to view Chaucer as a master of poetic humour.

Others have viewed the narrator's actions as part of a ploy within the fictional world of the poem to encourage the knight to keep talking, or as a means of breaking up what might otherwise be a rather long explanation. But as Helen Cooper points out, what strikes some readers as peculiar behaviour on the dreamer's part is consistent with the conventions of dream poetry, not to mention the experience of dreams themselves, whose origins and meanings were as mysterious in the Middle Ages as they are today.[40] As the hen Pertelote tells the rooster Chauntecleer in the *Nun's Priest's Tale*, dreams could be divine revelations, portents or warnings concerning the future; extensions of the dreamer's conscious life; or perhaps merely the meaningless consequences of 'replecciouns [overeating]' (2923), in which case they were best dealt with by taking 'som laxatyf' (2943). This ambiguity only added to the sense of dreams' potential displacement from the realities of lived experience and made dream poems a space in which the imagination could roam free. Consequently, there was no 'need' for the narrators of gnomic or potentially meaningless dream poems to be carefully distanced from their subject-matter – after all, their poems purportedly only concerned dreams, whose content could mask any sort of meaning, or carry no meaning at all.

Regardless of *why* the narrator of *The Book of the Duchess* behaves as he does, his behaviour reveals him to be a fish out of water in the knight's courtly, tragic world – he is out of his emotional depth, unable to fully grasp or properly share in such aristocratic sorrow. As the dream draws to an end, the narrator's reply to the knight's blunt explanation that his lover is dead seems almost purposely, pointedly, insufficient, but it is also final: 'Is that youre los? Be God, hyt ys routhe! [Is that your loss? By God, it is a pity!]' (1310). There is no more to be said, and no more that *can* be said by someone in Chaucer's position to someone like Gaunt. The narrator's words break the dream's spell: as if on cue, a distant horn sounds the conclusion of the hunt, as the narrator observes that 'al was doon,/ For that tyme, the hert-huntyng [all was done, for that time, the hart-/heart-hunting]' (1312–13).

With the word *hert* (which can refer to either a 'hart'/deer or a 'heart'), Chaucer deftly folds the soundscape of the dream and the narrator's conversation with the black knight together. A further series of puns and clues connects the dreamworld of his poem to the events of his own time and place: the hunt returns to 'A long castel with walles white,/ Be Seynt Johan, on a ryche hil [A long castle with walls white, by Saint John, on a rich hill]' (1319–20). Hidden in this wordplay are clues to the poem's true subject: *long castel* recalls Gaunt's position as Duke of Lancaster (also referred to as 'Loncastel' or 'Longcastell'), while the phrase *walles white* seems to be a veiled reference to Blanche herself. The fact that the castle is situated *be Seynt Johan* (Gaunt's name-saint) and on a *ryche hil* (a nod to Gaunt's earldom of Richmond) makes it abundantly clear of whom and to whom Chaucer is writing.[41]

* * *

With its sleep-deprived narrator, its wordplay and its misdirection, *The Book of the Duchess* announces Chaucer's skill, not only as a young poet capable of mastering one of the most popular genres of the Middle Ages, but as a writer capable of deftly weaving play and consolation together in a single text. It is a poem that is perfectly suited to the elegance and fashions of the courtly environment in which Chaucer found himself. *The Book of the Duchess* also invites us to reflect on what it was like for Chaucer to navigate the exalted social circles in which he moved during his twenties, and how his writing might even have aided him in this delicate task. Several of Chaucer's other works show traces of his connections to historical figures great and small, and it seems likely that some of these individuals may have formed part of an intimate circle of acquaintances with whom Chaucer shared his writing. Though no manuscripts survive that can be definitively identified as the product of his own hand, some of his poems speak or refer directly to these individuals, while others feature what are supposed to be fictional avatars of people Chaucer knew (or perhaps hoped to know better).

The Book of the Duchess may not have been the first time that Chaucer's aristocratic connections provided inspiration or even possible patronage of his poems. It has been suggested, for example, that Blanche may have commissioned Chaucer's *ABC to the Virgin*, although the only evidence for this is a remark in Thomas Speght's 1602 edition of the poem, which states that it was composed 'at the request of Blanche, Duchesse of Lancaster, as a praier for her privat use'.[42] Nor would *The Book of the Duchess* be the last time that Chaucer's poetry would be connected with English royalty. *The House of Fame* and *The Parliament of Fowls* may have been inspired by ongoing marriage negotiations on behalf of Richard II. And the benevolent but stern figure of Alceste in the prologue to Chaucer's *Legend of Good Women* has been linked to Richard's eventual bride, Anne of Bohemia, perhaps as part of a panegyric counterpoint to Chaucer's translation of *Le Roman de la rose* and his depiction of Criseyde in *Troilus and Criseyde*.[43] These later works and the illustrious figures to whom they have been connected suggest that Chaucer's first major poem made a very good first impression indeed.

THREE

Finding His Voice

In the library of the University of Pennsylvania is a manuscript now known as MS Codex 902. Datable to around 1400, the manuscript is a collection of poems by a number of French poets, some of whom Chaucer knew personally, and some of whom influenced his own writing, including Guillaume de Machaut (c. 1300–1377), Eustache Deschamps (c. 1346–c. 1406) and the dashing Savoyard Oton de Granson (d. 1397), with whom Chaucer was very likely friends.[1] The manuscript is not particularly lavish; its plain parchment pages are filled with French poems neatly written in two columns of spiky brown script. The poems – which were written by more than one hand – are interspersed with such headings as 'Balade' and 'Rondel', written in red ink. But if one looks closely, another inscription can be seen alongside fifteen of the poems: 'Ch'.

The meaning of the initials is unclear. They were added in after the manuscript was written, and it seems unlikely that they were intended as abbreviations for *chanson* or *chant*.[2] Might they be attempts to identify the author? And, if so, might 'Ch' be a reference to 'Chaucer'?

It is certainly possible. While Chaucer would eventually become known as the father of *English* poetry, it is more than likely that his earliest poetic efforts were in French, the fashionable language of the court circles in which he moved during the early part of his career. The likely date of composition for the poems is around 1360, which would coincide with Chaucer's early court service.[3] Other clues within the manuscript suggest that MS Codex 902 may have been assembled by Chaucer's associate Granson, a nobleman who was also acquainted with John of Gaunt and who served the English Crown on and off between 1369 and his death in 1397. It has been suggested that 'correspondences between several of their poems point to an artistic partnership' between Chaucer and Granson.[4] Did that partnership lead Granson to include Chaucer's French poems alongside his own in MS Codex 902?

Whether or not Chaucer was the author of the 'Ch' poems, MS Codex 902 is a material reminder of the cultural influences that dominated the early years of Chaucer's life, and of English's relative lack of prestige in comparison with the literary languages of continental Europe. At this point in time, English was not even a terribly prestigious language within England's borders. Edward III's court was so thoroughly francophone that the French-speaking chronicler and poet Jean Froissart (c. 1337–c. 1405) 'apparently never troubled to learn English' during his time there.[5] The dominant languages of medieval English legal culture were Latin and French, while the language of the Church was Latin.[6] The multilingual landscape of fourteenth-century England is reflected in its poetry – Chaucer's contemporary and personal acquaintance John Gower (c. 1330–1408), for example, wrote poetry in Latin, French and English.

Because he spent so much of his early life serving in aristocratic and royal households, most of Chaucer's earliest literary experiences would have been French, not only in terms of their language but in terms of their form, content and style. Despite the hostilities of the Hundred Years' War, French literature and culture were fashionable, even in England. At the same time, Italian influence was beginning to be felt in English literary culture; the regular stream of visitors from the Continent placed the

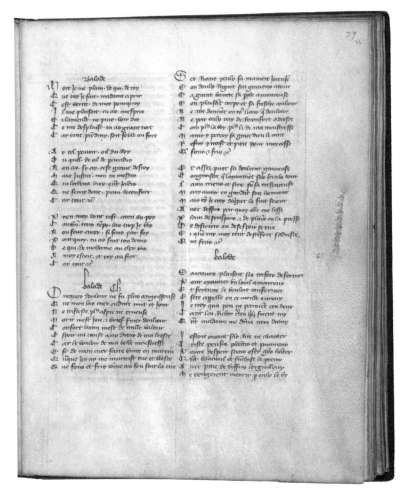

Folio featuring the 'Ch' inscription in the bottom half of the left-hand column from the University of Pennsylvania [Chansonnier] manuscript, 1400.

English court at the fringes of a network including such figures as Philippe de Mézières and other participants in 'intellectual exchange, potential "carriers" of Italian culture'.[7] Consequently, despite England's relative geographic isolation and its ongoing war with France, it continued to engage in regular cultural exchanges that traversed borders and even enemy lines.

Chaucer's royal service and the Continental travels he undertook at intervals over the course of his career shaped not only his professional life but his writing. Perhaps most significantly, these experiences would have made it impossible for Chaucer to escape the reality of English's lowly status relative to the sophistication of French literature and the classically informed ambitions of Italian literary culture. If humorous misdirection and self-deprecation helped Chaucer to compensate for his relatively humble social position in an early work like *The Book of the Duchess*, they also helped him counterbalance – and even exploit – English's relatively humble status in comparison with its Continental counterparts. In the end, Chaucer developed a poetic style that rivalled the literary achievements of medieval France and Italy while remaining, at its heart, distinctively English.

Continental Styles

Given that English is currently the most widely spoken language in the world, it is difficult now to have a clear sense of what it meant for Chaucer to write in English in the late fourteenth century. David Wallace has observed rather bluntly that, 'viewed from continental European perspectives, Chaucer's England and its poetry appear both eccentric and retarded':

> Its eccentricity is geographical: from classical times
> onward, the British Isles had been mapped as the
> last stop before *ultima Thule* and the end of the world.
> In Boccaccio's *Decameron* 11, 3, England is regarded
> as more exotic and fantastical than Barbary . . . The
> vernaculars of these distant islands were thus seen
> as eccentric and of scant literary consequence.[8]

Even if we acknowledge the (slight) degree to which Chaucer's work was appreciated in his own time by such writers as Granson or Deschamps, he was not writing in a language that was considered to be of great literary significance.[9] As Ardis Butterfield has noted, 'If, from the hindsight of history, Chaucer appears as the great father figure of English literature, from the perspective of the late fourteenth century, he appears as a rare example of otherwise small-scale English brilliance in the powerfully substantial production of medieval writings in French.'[10] In other words, while medieval English people consumed Continental literature both at home and during their travels on the Continent, cultural influence tended to flow towards their island rather than away from it.

The scale of French influence on English literature can be glimpsed in the variety of French sources on which Chaucer drew when writing *The Book of the Duchess*. The poem's opening derives from the first twelve lines of Froissart's *Paradys d'amours* (the correspondence between the two passages is very nearly word for word).[11] Much of its content is inspired by such French poems as Machaut's *La fonteinne amoureuse*, *Le jugement dou Roy de Behaingne* and *Le remède de fortune*,[12] and some of the very first images the dreamer describes are the walls of his dream-bedroom that 'with colours fyne/ Were peynted, bothe text and glose,/ Of al the Romaunce of the Rose [with fine colours were painted, both text and gloss, with all the *Romance of the Rose*]' (332–4). This is one of many Chaucerian allusions to the thirteenth-century *Roman de la rose*, one of the most influential works of medieval secular literature.

If French literature had long held sway both in England and on the Continent, the fourteenth century bore witness to new achievements in Italian literature that would have a tremendous impact on literature throughout Europe in the centuries to come. Dante Alighieri (d. 1321) put both Italy and the Italian language on the medieval literary map with the *Divina Commedia* (Divine Comedy, completed *c.* 1320), poetic proof that great literature could be written in the vernacular as well as in Latin. Other Italian intellectuals and poets such as Francesco Petrarca (1304–1374) – known in English as Petrarch – and Giovanni Boccaccio contributed to a revival of classical learning and culture that would come to be known as humanism, and which would take hold in England roughly a century later.

If Chaucer's poetry was influenced by that of his French and Italian contemporaries, so were his notions of what it meant to be a poet. In the Middle Ages, the title of 'author' was almost exclusively reserved for classical writers, the Church Fathers or God himself ('the divine *auctor*').[13] Likewise, the word 'poet' was applied most commonly to 'ancient writers' or 'authorities', rather than to living writers.[14] But by Chaucer's lifetime, there were signs that this was beginning to change. In 1341, Petrarch was awarded the status of poet laureate and crowned with laurel leaves in Rome, the *città eterna* (eternal city). Decades later, Chaucer would refer to Petrarch's laureate status in the prologue to *The Clerk's Tale*, whose narrator claims to have learned the story 'at Padowe of a worthy clerk [at Padua from a worthy clerk]' (27): 'Frauuceys Petrak, the lauriat poete . . . whos rethorike sweete/ Enlumyned al Ytaille of poetrie [Francis Petrarch, the laureate poet, whose sweet rhetoric illuminated all of Italy with poetry]' (31–3). For Chaucer, Petrarch was an example of the exalted status a poet could achieve in his own lifetime. At the same time, Dante's poetic achievements in Italian must have suggested to Chaucer that similar heights could be reached in other vernaculars, perhaps even one as humble as English.

Travel in the Fourteenth Century

While Chaucer encountered many French and Italian literary masterpieces during his early years of service, the journeys he made between England and the Continent over the course of his lifetime enabled him to visit some of the most important cultural capitals of medieval Europe.

Travel of one kind or another was a common feature of life in medieval Europe. Craftsmen might travel to cities to gain apprenticeships that would improve their skills. Poets and minstrels might travel from household to household (or, if they were a little more fortunate, *with* a particular household) in the hope of earning a living. Merchants moved back and forth across the Continent, the Mediterranean and the English Channel to acquire and sell their wares. Men and women from all walks of life went on pilgrimages to the Holy Land and numerous sacred sites for the sake of their souls, and sometimes for the sake of adventure. Missionaries travelled in order to convert, crusaders to conquer. Diplomats travelled from one place to another to uphold their nations' interests.

The mode by which people travelled in the Middle Ages varied according to class and gender. Medieval people crossed rivers and small bodies of water by ferry, and larger bodies of water by ship. When journeying overland, they might travel on foot, on horseback, in carts or wagons, or (for the very wealthy indeed) in carriages, though the lack of springs probably made riding in a carriage along bumpy roads rather uncomfortable.[15] If a person was riding on horseback, the type of horse that person was riding would often be determined by its rider's wealth, gender and station in life, as well as the specific use to which the horse was being put – there was 'the great war-horse (charger or destrier), the secondary war horse, the rouncey [an all-purpose horse], then the palfrey of the ladies, cart-horse (pack-horse), the sumpter horse [a type of pack horse], and the hubby (used for skirmishes by light cavalry), to mention just the most important types'.[16]

As the *General Prologue* of Chaucer's *Canterbury Tales* demonstrates, one's horse could be a living, breathing symbol not only of one's rank and wealth but of one's personality, a fact that Chaucer exploits to great effect in his descriptions of the *Canterbury Tales* pilgrims. The Monk, for example, sits astride a palfrey (a valuable smaller, lighter-weight horse ideal for covering great distances), a mount that, along with the jingling bells of its bridle, would have been quite a showy status symbol for a man of the Church. By contrast, the impoverished Clerk rides a horse that is as lean as he is ('As leene was his horse as is a rake', while the Clerk 'looked holwe [hollow], and therto sobrely [abstemious]' (287–9)).[17]

The fact that travel was such an integral part of many medieval people's lives did not mean it was without its dangers. Anyone travelling on the road ran the risk of being robbed or assaulted. Surviving records indicate that in 1390 Chaucer himself was robbed by highwaymen in Kent during a journey that was likely connected with his employment as Clerk of the King's Works (the robbers relieved him of not only money and various possessions but also his horse).[18] Because medieval travellers were largely responsible for their own safety, they frequently sought to travel with companions.[19] Even this was no guarantee of safe passage: the book that describes the travels of early fifteenth-century mystic and pilgrim Margery Kempe notes that she was abandoned by her travelling companions while journeying to Aachen, and that she later encountered English pilgrims who had been robbed of their money.[20]

Voyaging by sea had its own dangers, from which many travellers hoped to be protected through divine intervention. The 'special devotees' of St Leonard, for instance, included 'travelers overseas, fishermen, and all who were specifically concerned with protection from drowning and safe return from the sea'.[21] A reference to St Leonard in *The House of Fame* suggests that Chaucer was familiar with the cult of the saint. Chaucer describes himself as falling asleep and entering the dreamworld of *The House of Fame*, 'As he that wery was forgo/ On pilgrymage myles two/ To the corseynt Leonard,/ To make lythe of that was hard [as he who was thoroughly exhausted on a 2-mile pilgrimage to St Leonard, to make easy what was hard]' (112–18). Chaucer may have made just such a visit to a shrine in the summer of 1378, when he was returning from a trip to Lombardy as part of a delegation meeting with Barnabò Visconti, Duke of Milan.[22] On his return to England, he would have disembarked at Hythe in Kent and made his way to the Norman Church of St Leonard 3 kilometres (2 mi.) away to offer thanks for his safe passage across the sea.

Domestic travel was also a regular part of life for medieval people. Within England, the devastation caused by the Black Death and the refusal of many landowners to raise wages encouraged young people to relocate in order to seek better pay (though legislation such as the 1351 Statute of Labourers sought to prevent this).[23] Until the strictures of the Reformation took hold, pilgrimage would continue to be a popular reason (or excuse) for local and international travel well into the sixteenth century.

The frequency with which later medieval people travelled is reflected in Chaucer's *Canterbury Tales*, whose premise is a pilgrimage from Southwark in London to the shrine of Thomas Becket at Canterbury Cathedral. Several of its characters are described as well travelled in the *General Prologue*, including the Wife of Bath:

> thries hadde she been at Jerusalem;
> She hadde passed many a straunge strem;
> At Rome she hadde been, and at Boloigne,

In Galice at Seint-Jame, and at Coloigne.
She koude muchel of wandrynge by the weye.

   thrice had she been to Jerusalem;
She had crossed many a foreign sea;
At Rome she had been, and at Boulogne;
In Galicia at St James [of Compostela], and at Cologne.
She knew much of wandering by the way.
(463–7)

As this list of famous destinations makes clear, this is far from
being the Wife's first pilgrimage, though the rather tongue-in-
cheek remark that she knows a great deal about 'wandering' hints
that her motives for going on these pilgrimages may not have
been entirely pure (as Helen Cooper tactfully notes, 'wives pro-
verbially used pilgrimages as a cover for other activities').[24] For
his part, the Knight has been involved in a number of military
campaigns abroad:

Ful worthy was he in his lordes werre,
And therto hadde he riden, no man ferre,
As wel in cristendom as in hethenesse,
And evere honoured for his worthynesse;
At Alisaundre he was whan it was wonne.
Ful ofte tyme he hadde the bord bigonne
Aboven all nacions in Pruce;
In Lettow hadde he reysed and in Ruce,
No Cristen man so ofte of his degree.
In Gernade at the seege eek hadde he be
Of Algezir, and riden in Belmarye.
At Lyeys was he and at Satalye,
Whan they were wonne, and in the Grete See
At many a noble armee hadde he be.

At mortal batailles hadde he been fiftene,
And foughten for oure feith at Tramyssene
In lystes thries, and ay slayn his foo.
This ilke worthy knyght hadde been also
Somtyme with the lord of Palatye
Agayn another hethen in Turkye.

He was very worthy in his lord's war,
And for that reason he had ridden, no man farther,
In Christendom as well as in heathen lands,
And was always honoured for his worthiness;
He was at Alexandria when it was won.
He had sat in the place of honour very many times,
Above all the knights of every nation in Prussia;
In Lithuania he had campaigned, and in Russia,
No Christian man of his rank as often.
He had also been in Granada at the siege
Of Algeciras, and had ridden in Benmarin [Morocco].
He was at Ayash and at Atalia
When they were won, and in the Mediterranean
He had been on many a noble expedition.
He had been in fifteen battles to the death,
And fought for our faith at Tlemcen
Three times in formal duels, and always had slain his foe.
This same worthy knight had also been
At one time with the lord of Balat
Against another heathen in Turkey.
(47–66)

This catalogue of campaigns and foreign battles maps out the limits of the Christian world as it stood in the later fourteenth century. It would be an ambitious itinerary for a modern traveller, let alone a medieval English knight.

Chaucer Abroad

As he entered his thirties, Chaucer was undertaking a number of trips abroad in the service of the king. It is unclear precisely how important a role he played on these occasions, but whatever the circumstances, between 1372 and 1387 he was party to negotiations abroad relating to trade, diplomacy and the arrangement of a royal marriage. On these trips, Chaucer had the opportunity to see Continental literature from a new perspective, one that would shape his own future literary projects.

On 1 December 1372, Chaucer received an advance of 100 marks (or £66 13s 4d) to undertake a journey overseas 'on the secret business of the lord king'.[25] After receiving this payment, Chaucer set out on what was likely his first trip to Italy, bound for Genoa (a seaport in northwestern Italy) and Florence. He was to participate in negotiations with the Genoese for the construction of a new English seaport for their merchants (though political or military discussions may also have taken place). It was a delicate mission, not least because of the growing outrage in London and Calais concerning the sale of licences to Italian merchants and others that enabled them to avoid paying trade duties in staple towns (designated places for the collection of duties related to overseas trade).

It would not have been an easy journey. In order to get to their destination, Chaucer's party would have had to cross the Channel and journey over the Alps via the Great St Bernard Pass, all in the depths of winter. While the pass was the oldest route over the Pennine Alps, the narrow, winding roads and the bone-chilling cold made it extremely perilous.[26] The travellers may well have stopped at the hospice at the pass to rest. Founded in the eleventh century by St Bernard of Menthon, the hospice is better known now as the summer residence of the famous St Bernard dogs that bear his name. After the pass,

Chaucer's road likely took him and his companions through Aosta and Turin before they finally arrived at the port city of Genoa.

Fourteenth-century Italy was very different from the country we know today. Instead of a unified nation, the peninsula consisted of a jumble of independent city states, republics, dictatorships and principalities that were not infrequently at odds (or at war) with one another. At the same time, when Chaucer was visiting it, 'Italy was the heart of Europe, physical witness to the grandeurs of imperial Rome and the origins of the Christian church . . . and perhaps two centuries ahead of England in terms of artistic and literary innovation.'[27]

It was in this vibrant cultural scene that Chaucer was immersed during his time in Italy. Florence, which Chaucer visited in 1373, must have particularly impressed him after his trip to Genoa. The birthplace of Dante, Florence was the beating heart of poetic achievement in fourteenth-century Italy. But while it is possible that Chaucer met such luminaries as Petrarch and Boccaccio on his visit, most scholars agree that it is unlikely he did so. Nevertheless, in Florence,

> Chaucer was at the centre of the literary cult of Dante; lectures on the poet had been established, and the next year's series were due to be given by Boccaccio. [Chaucer] had heard of the *Divine Comedy*, from Italian merchants and bankers in London; now he was able to take home a memory of reading the great poem, or even carry away a manuscript of it, or part of it, and so make his journey really worth while.[28]

This image of a young English writer and royal attendant eager to meet or at the least learn from the work of other poets is an appealing one. It is possible that Chaucer managed to acquire manuscripts of works by Italian writers during his travels, or that he heard or read enough to bring memories of the texts back to England with him. And it is tempting to picture him as someone whose diplomatic mission on this trip might have been related to trade or politics, but whose real interest lay in the literary culture he could absorb while he was there and perhaps take home with him when he left. However, it is difficult to guess the extent to which this might have been the case. Chaucer was still very much on the fringes of court life and courtly culture, and the majority of his poetic career lay ahead of him. What *does* seem likely is that his trip to Italy changed his perception of what poetry could do, and what poets could be. Seeing the esteem in which Dante, Petrarch and Boccaccio were held in their homeland must have made a great impression on him. He would have witnessed the reverence with which these poets and their works were treated, both as keepers of classical tradition and as those responsible for establishing powerful new literary traditions in the vernacular. This was something very different from the world of courtly literature he had known in England and during his travels in France. But was it something that Chaucer could export to England and replicate in English?

When he had written *The Book of the Duchess*, Chaucer had been writing for a relatively small and specific audience on a very specific occasion. Even later in his literary career, copies of his work do not seem to have circulated beyond a small group of readers. No manuscripts of Chaucer's poetry can be dated with certainty to his lifetime, though a handful are datable to within a decade or two after his death.[29] During his travels on the Continent, and particularly during his travels in Italy, Chaucer would have encountered ambitious poetry whose influence was already sending ripples throughout the literary world. But just as self-deprecation and surprise had helped him navigate the delicate circumstances surrounding his composition of *The Book of the*

Duchess, so they would also help him as he took his next steps as a poet.

From Florence to *The House of Fame*

As *The Book of the Duchess* makes clear, Chaucer was already capable of using humour to suit his poetry and his poetic voice to a socially superior audience and a potentially daunting poetic tradition. And it may be that, in the process of writing *The Book of the Duchess*, Chaucer found that dream poetry lent itself particularly well to his poetic aims. Within the fiction of dream poems, neither authors nor dreamer-narrators were responsible for what they described. More importantly, within dream poetry, *dreams* – not personal ambitions – were what prompted the act of writing itself.

Chaucer exploited these qualities to pave the way for his poetic ambition in one of the texts he almost certainly composed after his first travels to Italy: *The House of Fame* (likely written sometime between 1374 and 1385). In this poem, Chaucer grapples with the formidable legacy of Italian literature by displacing his own poetic ambitions onto a slightly absurd dreamer avatar. The poem begins with its narrator's reflections on dreams and their significance (or lack thereof), after which – upon falling asleep – the narrator is eventually transported by an eagle to the palace of the goddess Fame and the related house of Rumour in order to encounter tidings about which he can write.

The very structure of *The House of Fame*, split into three 'books', seems to be a nod to the tripartite structure of the *Divina Commedia*: *Inferno*, *Purgatorio* and *Paradiso*. The first words that the dreamer encounters are a further clue to Chaucer's ambitions: whereas in *The Book of the Duchess* the dreamer is confronted with the story of Troy and the 'text and glose/ Of al the Romaunce of the Rose [text and gloss of all the *Romance of the Rose*]'

(333–4), the first text to be referenced in *The House of Fame*'s dream is Virgil's *Aeneid*, the epic poem concerning the legendary roots of Italy's founding in the wake of the Trojan diaspora. The narrator of *The House of Fame* sees the famous first words of Virgil's poem engraved on a brass tablet in a temple dedicated to Venus: 'I wol now synge, yif I kan,/ The armes and also the man/ That first cam, thurgh his destinee,/ Fugityf of Troy contree [I will now sing, if I am able, of the warfare and also the man who first came, through his destiny, a fugitive of the country of Troy]' (143–6). Over more than three hundred lines, Chaucer provides a summary of Virgil's narrative, highlighting in particular Aeneas' eventual betrayal of Dido, one of many such betrayals recounted in classical texts. This is a significant deviation from the fashionable French poems that influenced *The Book of the Duchess*.

But if this Virgilian grandeur suggests that the poem is about to take a classical turn, subsequent events upend any such expectations. Chaucer's dreamer exits the temple only to be snatched up by a loquacious golden eagle. Readers of Dante's *Commedia* might recognize this as an allusion to the golden eagle that carries him into the heavens in its second *cantica*. Chaucer's eagle, however, strikes a more comical note, complaining about how difficult it is to carry the dreamer: 'Seynte Marye,/ Thou art noyous for to carye! [Saint Mary, thou art troublesome to carry!]' (573–4). After this rather humiliating start, the dreamer is compelled to listen to the eagle drone on for more than two hundred lines on such subjects as the nature of sound, which he describes as 'noght but air y-broken [nothing more than broken air]' (765). With this comparison of sound to breaking wind, Chaucer deflates the grandeur of his poem's Dantean scenario, effectively masking any aspiration to poetic greatness that he himself might have.

For all these comic twists on his source material, however, Chaucer still depicts himself as desirous of determining his own fame (however unlikely the poem's depiction of Fame might

suggest that to be). As he replies when asked if he has come to
Fame's palace to receive a good reputation,

> 'Nay, for sothe, frend,' quod y;
> 'I cam noght hyder, graunt mercy,
> For no such cause, by my hed!
> Sufficeth me, as I were ded,
> That no wight have my name in honde.
> I wot myself best how y stonde;
> For what I drye, or what I thynke,
> I will myselven al hyt drynke,
> Certeyn, for the more part,
> As fer forth as I kan myn art.'

> 'No, truly, friend,' I said;
> 'I did not come here, thank you,
> For any such purpose, by my head!
> It is enough for me, should I be dead,
> That no man should have my name in hand.
> I know best myself how I stand:
> For what I experience, or what I think,
> I will myself drink all of it,
> Certainly, for the most part,
> As much as I know how to practice my art.' (1873–82)

In these lines, we glimpse a writer who may be hesitant and self-
effacing in the shadow of his great Italian and classical forerunners,
but who is nonetheless determined to make his own way in the
literary world, as best he can.

Despite its narrator's self-deprecating tone, *The House of
Fame*, with its insistent gestures towards the poetic achievements
of writers past and present, is worlds away from *The Book of the
Duchess*. It is one of Chaucer's most important steps onto the

grand stage of literary tradition. Perhaps the poem's uncertainty regarding the reliability and durability of fame reflects Chaucer's sense of his own audacity. Perhaps it reflects his own uncertainty about whether any poem in English could accomplish so much. In the end, Chaucer did not complete this particular literary exper-iment. But although *The House of Fame* remained unfinished, its author's poetic career would accelerate in the years to come.

His Life's Work

Regardless of what his poetic ambitions may have been in the years that followed his travels to Genoa and Florence, Chaucer surely never could have predicted the course his literary career would take. His professional life would soon undergo equally sig-nificant changes with his appointment as a customs officer in June 1374, a development which would bring him back to the city of London, where he would take up residence above the gate of Aldgate. This was merely another in a series of career changes that Chaucer would experience throughout the rest of his life-time. But despite those twists and turns, he would go on to produce an impressive variety of poetry, as a later dream poem makes clear.

Likely begun a little over a decade after he composed *The House of Fame, The Legend of Good Women* is yet another of Chaucer's unfinished works.[30] Its prologue is the last dream vision Chaucer would write, and one he revised at least once – two versions exist: the 'F Prologue' and the 'G Prologue'. Though Chaucer had written some of his greatest poetry before he began work on the *Legend*, its narrator cuts just as unimpres-sive a figure as the dreamer in *The House of Fame*: he falls asleep outdoors while worshipping his favourite flower (the daisy) and then finds himself in a dreamworld where the God of Love chas-tises him for having written poems that supposedly discouraged people from falling in love. However, this accusation provides a

convenient occasion for both the series of 'legends' that follow
and a catalogue of the works Chaucer had already written by this
point in time:

> He made the book that hight the Hous of Fame,
> And eke the Deeth of Blaunche the Duchesse,
> And the Parlement of Foules, as I gesse,
> And al the love of Palamon and Arcite
> Of Thebes, thogh the storye ys knowen lyte;
> And many an ympne for your halydayes,
> That highten balades, roundels, virelayes;
> And, for to speke of other holynesse,
> He hath in prose translated Boece,
> And maad the lyf also of Seynt Cecile.
> He made also, goon ys a gret while,
> Origenes upon the Maudelyne.

> He made the book that is called the *House of Fame*,
> And also the *Death of Blanche the Duchess*,
> And the *Parliament of Fowls*, as I suppose,
> And the whole love of Palamon and Arcite
> Of Thebes, though the story is little known;
> And many a hymn for your holidays,
> That are called ballads, roundels, virelays;
> And, to mention another religion,
> He has in prose translated *Boece*,
> And also made the life of Saint Cecilia.
> He also made, a long time ago,
> Origenes upon the Magdalene. (F 417–28)

Absurd and cowering, the *Legend*'s dreamer is nevertheless a fictional representation of a poet who was by now at the height of
his powers. And as is clear from the list of writings he provides,

Chaucer's body of work already comprised a dizzying variety of genres, subjects and forms.

By the middle of the 1380s, Chaucer was in his forties. He was both a seasoned traveller and a seasoned poet, one who had come into contact with some of the most sophisticated cultural centres of later medieval Europe. He had put that experience to good use, having already written what would eventually constitute the bulk of his known literary output. He had literary models to whose level he hoped someday to rise. The works he had already completed demonstrate not only the impact of travel and cultural exchange on his writing but the skills that brought him to the peak of his poetic career during the first of the two royal successions that he would witness during his lifetime.

FOUR

Custom and Craft

I n the accounts kept by the Keeper of the Wardrobe of the King's Household between June 1371 and 1373, 'Galfrido Chaucer' is one of several dozen squires of the king's chamber who received money to be used for the purchase of winter and summer robes.[1] This was not the first time Chaucer had received such a payment during his service in the king's household, but it is noteworthy for its identification of Chaucer as a squire of the king's *chamber*, specifically. In earlier documents he is referred to as an *esquier* (squire) or as an *esquier de greindre estat* (squire of less degree).[2] The identification of Chaucer as a squire of the king's chamber suggests that he had become a member of the king's inner household or *secreta familia*, a privileged position indeed for the son of a London wine merchant.[3]

By this point in his career, Chaucer's connections had brought him many advantages, not the least of which was his association with John of Gaunt. Chaucer had also taken his first ambitious steps as a poet, and his contact with Italian literary culture had given him new ideas about what poets could achieve, and what their cultural significance could be.

It was at this moment that Chaucer's life took a new turn, one that brought him away from the day-to-day activity of the royal household and into the bustling urban spaces of fourteenth-century London. In June 1374, he was appointed controller of the wool custom and wool subsidy and of the petty custom in the Port of London.[4] Although no record of the actual oath Chaucer took has been found, an oath of controller of petty custom for London dated to around 1376 charges the oath-taker, either 'in person or by suitable deputy for whom you will answer', to ensure that appropriate customs charges were paid in the Port of London, and to keep necessary records to ensure that the king was not defrauded or cheated out of any of these charges.[5] This new job required Chaucer to ensure that the weighing of wool exports and the collection of wool duties went smoothly. Above all, he had to ensure the honesty of customs collectors and the safe transmission of the duties they collected into the king's coffers.[6] This was a position of trust and responsibility, 'a not inconsequential position within [medieval England's] taxation apparatus' that would have required Chaucer to keep records of massive amounts of trade and payments in his own hand.[7] While one scholar claims to have discovered a document written by Chaucer himself during his years as a customs officer, the identification is far from certain, and Chaucer's handwritten records of the duties he collected during his tenure have yet to be found.[8]

It is unclear whether this new position was one that Chaucer had coveted or whether it was one that was imposed on him. Chaucer may have been carefully manoeuvred into position as controller by powerful people seeking to shore up their influence or line their pockets.[9] It has also been suggested that the move was simply a natural consequence of Chaucer's family connections with trade.[10] Chaucer may or may not have already possessed the accountancy skills needed to perform such a role successfully. But regardless of why he was given the post, he would hold it for more than a decade, during which he had ample time to acquire daily hands-on experience of the innermost workings of English taxation and trade.

The fluency Chaucer acquired in these matters shines through in the language of *The Shipman's Tale*, in which a merchant's wife agrees to exchange sex with a monk in return for money. The tale concludes with a pun on the word 'taillynge' (434), a word that variously signifies 'tallying', intercourse ('tailing') and the telling of tales ('taling'). Chaucer's description of the merchant's professional activities reflects his own familiarity with that kind of work and its accompanying vocabulary:

> this marchant up ariseth,
> And on his nedes sadly hym avyseth,
> And up into his countour-hous gooth he
> To rekene with hymself, wel may be,
> Of thilke yeer how that it with hym stood,
> And how that he despended hadde his good,
> And if that he encressed were or noon.
> His bookes and his bagges many oon
> He leith biforn hym on his countyng-bord.
> Ful riche was his tresor and his hord,
> For which ful faste his countour-dore he shette;
> And eek he nolde that no man sholde hym lette
> Of his acountes, for the meene tyme;
> And thus he sit til it was passed pryme.

> this merchant up arises
> And seriously considers his business,
> And he goes up into his counting-house
> To reckon with himself, as it may well be,
> Of that same year how things stood with him,
> And how he had spent his money,
> And if he had made a profit or not.
> His account-books and his moneybags, many a one,
> He lays before him on his counting-board,
> His treasure and his hoard were very rich,
> Consequently he shut his counting-house door very tightly,

> And also he did not want any man to prevent him
> From keeping his accounts, for the time being;
> And thus he sits until it was past nine o'clock. (75–88)

This sort of accounting and record-keeping was part of Chaucer's daily life as a customs officer, just as it had been part of his father's work as a vintner.

Chaucer's new position also meant a move back to London. In May 1374, he took up rent-free lodgings above the gate in Aldgate, the lease for which was initially intended to last for his entire life.[11] These lodgings consisted of rooms built along the top of the gate, as well as a cellar beneath. As one of London's city gates, Aldgate would have been a busy, noise-filled place during the daytime, with people, animals and goods regularly passing through. It was also a key part of London's city defences, fortified and manned by watchmen in time of war or when social disturbances threatened, as they would a few years later in 1381, when the rebels connected with the Peasants' Revolt broke into the city through Aldgate. But though the uprising was still years away, uncertainty and change were already in the air.

Uncertainty

On 21 September 1371, John of Gaunt (by now a 31-year-old widower) married the seventeen-year-old Constance (Costanza) of Castile, daughter of the late King Pedro of Castile (also known as Pedro the Cruel). The marriage may well have been prompted by Gaunt's ambitions, since it held out the possibility that he might be able to claim the throne of Castile. But it did not bring an end to his ongoing affair with Katherine Swynford, nor would it achieve the desired outcome: after great expense and loss of life, Gaunt's quest for Castilian kingship would ultimately end in failure in 1389.[12]

Gaunt's remarriage took place not long after a major event within the royal family: the death of his mother, Queen Philippa, at Windsor Castle in August 1369.[13] A writ of allowance from 1 September 1369 provides some indication of the scale of the public mourning that took place. Hundreds of members of the royal household and the aristocracy were granted gifts of black cloth. Dozens of servants, minstrels and even 'lavenders' (launderers) were granted smaller gifts of black cloth, as were the fifty 'poor women' who remained around the body and 'twelve poor men' who held torches around it. Both Chaucer and his wife, Philippa (who had served in the queen's household), are recorded as receiving gifts of black cloth for the occasion, and may have been present.[14]

Edward III, by now in his late fifties, had for three years been keeping a young mistress: Alice Perrers, who was younger than the king by several decades (and eight years younger than Gaunt).[15] The king's mistress was unpopular, all the more so in the years following the queen's death, when Perrers seemed to be exerting

John of Gaunt dining with the king of Portugal, miniature from a manuscript of Jean de Wavrin's *Anciennes et nouvelles chroniques d'Angleterre*, c. 1470–80.

ever more influence on the widowed king. Tensions ultimately came to a head in the so-called Good Parliament of 1376, at which Gaunt was compelled to stand in for the ailing king. Though the Good Parliament resulted in Perrers's temporary exile from court, it did nothing to reduce Gaunt's own unpopularity among the commoners, many of whom were convinced that he had designs on the English throne.

It was during these parliamentary proceedings that misfortune again struck the royal household. On 8 June 1376, the Black Prince finally succumbed to the illness that had steadily weakened him over eight years.[16] Popular to the last, he had carried the hopes of the nation on his shoulders. He left behind his son, Richard, who, at not yet ten years old, was now heir to the throne. In the Middle Ages, such a situation boded ill; as an old English proverb put it, 'Wo to thee, thou lond, whos king is a child [Woe to thee, thou land, whose king is a child]'.[17] Among the many reasons why a prospective child-king was a source of worry was the fact that his adult advisors and relatives might seek to take the throne for themselves. This seems to have been the concern with regard to Gaunt, though 'there is no hard evidence that he ever considered trying to subvert the line of succession'. Nevertheless, it was likely due to this concern that, within a few weeks of the Black Prince's death, Richard was brought before Parliament to be endowed with the title of Prince of Wales, a title that since 1301 had been given to the heir apparent to the English throne.[18]

Edward III's health continued to deteriorate after his son's death, though he was occasionally able to attend official events. On 23 April 1377, for example, the king was present at a ceremony in which two of his grandsons were admitted to the Order of the Garter: Prince Richard and his cousin, Henry Bolingbroke. But on 21 June 1377, just over a year after the Black Prince's death, Edward III passed away. His body was transferred from

Sheen Palace to London in a three-day procession, during which some 1,700 torches were used.[19] His funeral took place at Westminster Abbey on 5 July 1377, after which he was buried in the south side of the chapel of St Edward the Confessor, near his beloved queen. Edward III's fifty-year reign had finally come to an end.

A New King

It is unclear whether Chaucer was present at Edward III's funeral, though it seems probable that he was absent from England on the king's business at the time of Edward's death.[20] The king's passing may well have raised urgent questions for Chaucer about his future: would his connections at court still be useful? Would *he* still be considered useful to the new king and those around him?

English subjects likely had pressing questions of their own. Any change of regime brings with it uncertainty about the future, never more so than when the head of the new regime is entirely lacking in experience. The fact that the king-to-be was a boy of ten meant that, at least for a time, trusted men of experience would need to serve as his close advisors. However baseless they might have been, fears concerning Gaunt's rumoured designs on the throne ultimately meant that he was excluded from the proposed group of councillors, as was his younger brother, Thomas of Woodstock, Earl of Buckingham, though the two would continue to be involved in the governing of the kingdom.

Eleven days after his grandfather was buried, Richard was crowned king at Westminster Abbey. His was the first English coronation in fifty years, and it more than equalled the splendour of his grandfather's funeral. On the eve of his coronation, Richard processed from the Tower to Westminster, accompanied by representatives of the London wards, German mercenaries, Gascons

Richard II with his court after his coronation, miniature from a
manuscript of Jean de Wavrin's *Anciennes et nouvelles chroniques
d'Angleterre*, c. 1470–80.

and English earls, barons and knights, 'robed in white in honour
of the new king'.[21] John of Gaunt led the way, bearing the king's
sword, 'Curtana'.[22] The procession passed through the crowded
streets of Cheapside, Fleet Street and the Strand. The Cheapside
conduit 'flowed with wine' during the procession, and girls
dressed in white descended from a 'mock castle' further along the
route to offer Richard 'wine in gilt cups'. The following morning,
the king and his retinue processed from the palace at Westminster
to the abbey, where the king was conducted to 'a stage in the
centre of the church where his throne was placed'.[23] Accompanied
by choral singing, Richard made an offering and swore oaths to
uphold law and justice in the land, after which came the most

significant part of the coronation: the consecration, during which
Richard's shirt was removed and he was anointed on the hands,
chest, shoulders and head with holy oil:

> From this moment he was set apart from other mortals.
> He was God's anointed. He was not, as early medieval
> monarchs had considered themselves to be, the equivalent
> of a priest; but he was nevertheless endowed by the
> Almighty with special powers, the nature of which
> was made clear in the next part of the service when he
> was invested with the insignia of dominion. He was given
> the sword for the protection of the kingdom, the sceptre,
> 'the rod of the kingdom' and instrument for the correction
> of error, and the ring, 'the seal of holy faith' and symbol
> of his pastoral responsibilities. The boy king was then
> solemnly crowned.[24]

After the celebration of Mass, the solemnity of the coronation
gave way to festivity, as the king was carried from the abbey on
the shoulders of Sir Simon Burley. *The Westminster Chronicle*
notes rather grumpily that, owing to the jostling of the crowds,
the young king lost one of his shoes, which were made of red
velvet covered in fleurs-de-lis worked in pearls.[25] The shoes were
'part of the regalia worn by Alfred at his coronation in Rome by
Leo iv and later by Edward the Confessor at his coronation and
entrusted by Edward to Westminster Abbey', which accounts
for the irritated tone of this entry in the chronicle.[26]

A Hybrid Life

By the time the young Richard was getting to grips with his new
role as king, Chaucer had had several years to adapt to life in
the Custom House. Most of his days were spent in the counting

house, weighing room and docks of Wool Quay on the north bank of the Thames, on whose quays trade had taken place since the Roman age. In the thirteenth century, a new quay had been constructed in the area, which was replaced by 'a new well-built timber waterfront' when it collapsed sometime between the later thirteenth and mid-fourteenth centuries.[27] In 1382, the owner of the site, John Churchman, would construct a new Custom House 'for the quiet of Merchants . . . to serve for the tronage of wools in the Port of London', to which he would add an additional structure the following year: 'a small chamber for a latrine and a sollar over the counting house 38 feet long by 28½ feet broad, containing two chambers and a garret, as a further easement for the customers, controllers, and clerks'.[28] A timber drain uncovered during the twentieth-century excavation of the site was identified as a means of carrying sewage to the nearby Thames, and may even have been connected to a latrine used by Chaucer himself (or so archaeologists conjecture).[29]

The surviving fragments of the fourteenth-century structure that once stood on the site – not far from Chaucer's childhood home – hint at the various activities that took place within its walls: the counting of money, the weighing of goods and the keeping of accounts, as well as the everyday natural functions of the human bodies that worked in and visited the site. As records from this time indicate, this was a building that was filled with hustle and bustle, and with different kinds of people: any other controllers on site; the collectors, 'substantial merchants of the city of London' who collected the customs and kept half of the cocket seal (the other half of which was held by the controller); the 'troner and peser', responsible for weighing 'wool and other heavy commodities on a trone' (a large weighing device) and smaller items on scales; searchers to sniff out any unreported goods; and the packers and porters who carried items from place to place.[30] Chaucer would have overseen much of this work, and was required to keep accounts in his own hand. One can imagine that, after a busy day of management and paperwork, he might very well have returned to his lodgings above Aldgate somewhat 'daswed', as *The House of Fame* suggests.

Chaucer continued in this position through the death of Edward III and Richard's accession to the throne. One day after Edward III's death, and nearly a month before Richard's coronation, Chaucer was reappointed to his controllership, one of several reappointments made in five different ports on that day.[31] Not even the death of a king could bring the business of trade to a halt. Likewise, the late king's grants to Chaucer and other subjects were confirmed in Richard's name, as was customary in the event of a new king's accession to the throne. Chaucer's annuity was confirmed on 23 March 1378, and his grant of a daily pitcher of wine was commuted for an exchequer annuity of 20 marks on 18 April 1378.[32] Such transactions were a matter of bureaucratic routine, rather than the result of the young king's regard for Chaucer.

Despite his new responsibilities, Chaucer seems to have lived something of a hybrid life during his period as controller. While surviving documents do not indicate that he was ever again a member of the king's *secreta familia*, Chaucer's travels on the king's business continued. However, documentary evidence from within a few years of Chaucer's appointment to the controllership suggests that his work as a controller and his travel in service of the king were not always entirely compatible with one another. As early as 1377, Chaucer found it necessary to request deputies to replace him at the great and petty custom: an undated treasurer's bill indicates that Thomas Evesham, 'citizen of London' ('citein de Loundres'), was commissioned as Chaucer's deputy, and the commission was enrolled on 10 May 1377.[33] This seems to have been a temporary position, intended to cover the period of Chaucer's absence during his travels abroad on behalf of the king in May and June of that year. It would not be the last time a deputy controller was appointed during Chaucer's tenure in order to cover for his absence on the king's business: he appointed one Richard Barrett to act as his deputy controller from 16 May 1378, when Chaucer was 'to leave for foreign parts on the king's business'.[34] Barrett had been linked to the London custom house for more than a decade, which made him an ideal candidate to replace Chaucer on a temporary basis.[35]

A warrant dating from 13 May 1378 (three days before Barrett's appointment as Chaucer's deputy controller) indicates that on this occasion Chaucer accompanied Sir Edward de Berkeley on a journey to Lombardy 'for certain business touching our war' (possibly an attempt to secure military aid for England's ongoing war against France).[36] During his absence, Chaucer gave his power of attorney to a man named Richard Forester and to the poet John Gower. The letter transferring this power of attorney is the only documentary evidence we have concerning the relationship between the two poets, apart from references to one another in their works (some of which suggest their relationship may have soured at a later date).[37] Not long afterwards, Geoffrey travelled to France on a mission that concerned the fate of both his nation and the king himself: a journey to seek a treaty for peace between England and France, and to discuss a possible marriage between Richard and a daughter of his adversary in France.[38]

Chaucer continued to require deputies during the rest of his time in the controllership. Another temporary deputy, Henry Gisors, was appointed in June 1383 to carry out Chaucer's duties with respect to the wool custom and subsidy (the same Gisors would eventually succeed Chaucer as controller of the petty custom in 1386) because of Chaucer's need to conduct 'certain business', the exact nature of which is unknown.[39] In November 1384, Chaucer would again require a deputy during his absence for a month on 'some urgent business'. By February 1385, Chaucer had petitioned for a permanent deputy in the office of controller, and his petition was granted.[40]

The Craft of Poetry

Surviving documents from Chaucer's tenure as controller of customs suggest a life filled with comings and goings, paperwork and collaboration. He was working at the heart of English trade and taxation, and living in England's greatest city. At the same time, he was occasionally called away from this work to travel on royal business. In addition to all of this, Chaucer was now the father of several children: two sons, named Thomas (b. c. 1367) and Lewis (b. c. 1380), and possibly two daughters named Elizabeth and Agnes, though the extent to which Chaucer might have been directly involved in his children's upbringing was probably minimal.

Given how busy he was, it is remarkable that this period of Chaucer's life was also a period during which he was extremely active as a poet. It is hard to date any of Chaucer's works with much precision, but what work can be dated to the period of his controllership suggests that for Chaucer these were years of poetic experimentation. It may have been during his early years as a controller, for example, that he began work on the texts that would eventually become *The Second Nun's Tale* (a life of St Cecilia) and *The Monk's Tale*, a Boccaccian series of stories about the downfall of great men and women that, like *The House of Fame*, may have been partially inspired by his recent travels to Italy. Italian inspiration may also be seen in another poem dating from this period: his incomplete tragic love poem *Anelida and Arcite*, in which Anelida, queen of Armenia, is ultimately abandoned by her lover, the false Arcite. While the poem has largely been 'politely ignored' (as one scholar puts it), it deserves attention for what it reveals about Chaucer's development as a poet.[41]

The introductory portion of the poem draws on both Boccaccio's *Teseida* and Statius's *Thebaid*, but the love story that follows does not appear in either, and may have been Chaucer's own invention.[42] In terms of its form, *Anelida and Arcite* is also among the most intricately constructed poems Chaucer ever wrote: it incorporates five different types of stanza, including, possibly for the first time in English, 'rhyme royal' stanzas (seven-line stanzas of iambic pentameter, rhyming *ababbcc*).[43] The poem's experimentation with versification suggests that Chaucer's interest in imitating Continental poets extended to form as well as subject-matter and style.

It was during this period of experimentation that Chaucer wrote one of his most charming poems: *The Parliament of Fowls*, a dream poem in which Nature presides over a collection of birds who have gathered together to choose their mates: 'For this was on Seynt Valentynes day,/ Whan every foul cometh ther to chese his make [For this was on Saint Valentine's Day,/ When every bird comes there to choose his mate]' (309–10). It has been suggested that the *Parliament* may be the first poem written to commemorate St Valentine's Day as a celebration of love, and similar commemorations of the day may be found in the work of some of Chaucer's contemporaries, including Gower and Granson.[44]

At first, it appears that this avian mating ritual will proceed in an orderly fashion. Nature declares that the tercel eagle, 'The foul royal, above yow in degree [the royal bird whose rank is higher than yours]' (394), will be the first to choose his mate, after which the other birds will choose 'by order [in order of rank]' (400). But of course, the best-laid plans of mice, men and apparently birds often go awry. First, the eagles break out into an argument regarding which of them has the right to choose a beautiful female eagle perched on Nature's hand. The rest of the birds, impatient at the delay, subsequently argue about

which male eagle most deserves the female eagle, their squabble
intermingling human words with avian sounds:

> The goos, the cokkow, and the doke also
> So cryede, 'Kek kek! kokkow! quek, quek!' hye,
> That thourgh myne eres the noyse wente tho.
> The goos seyde, 'Al this nys not worth a flye!'

> The goose, the cuckoo, and also the duck
> Cried 'Kek, kek! Cuckoo! Quack, Quack!' so loudly,
> That the noise then went through my ears.
> The goose said, 'All of this is not worth a fly!' (498–501)

Given the uproar that results from the initially orderly mating
process, it is no wonder that in the end the female eagle asks
Nature to permit her to wait another year before making her
choice (perhaps hoping that the furore might have died down
by then).

While neither the date nor the intended audience of *The
Parliament of Fowls* can be identified with certainty, it is possible
that the poem represents the intersection of Chaucer's work as
a poet with his work in the service of the young Richard II. More
specifically, the poem may have been inspired by Chaucer's travels undertaken in pursuit of peace with France, peace that might
be secured by means of a betrothal. Marriage was a very common
way of resolving conflict between warring nations and families
in the Middle Ages. In Richard's case, marriage with a French
princess would also have been an excellent way of reinforcing
his claim to the French crown. A journey to France to discuss
such a marriage seems to have taken place sometime between
June 1377 and 6 March 1381, when payment for the journey
was issued. The issue roll entry that records a payment of £22 to
Chaucer by Richard II mentions both a journey to France 'in the

time of King Edward . . . for the sake of a peace treaty' ('tempore
Regis Edwardi . . . causa tractatus pacis') and a journey made
after Richard's accession to discuss the possible marriage.[45] Jean
Froissart noted Chaucer's presence at the latter negotiations,
which took place at Montreuil, some 70 kilometres (45 mi.) from
Calais: he records that one 'Jeffrois Cauchiés' was among those
representing the English side of the negotiations.[46]

Richard ultimately married Anne of Bohemia in Westminster
Abbey on 20 January 1382, despite the fact that 'there was a
German prince who had been betrothed to her for seven years
. . . and the French Dauphin had made a late bid'.[47] Given these
circumstances (as well as Chaucer's prior involvement in marriage
negotiations on behalf of the king), it is plausible that the ani-
mated avian debate at the heart of *The Parliament of Fowls* was
written at least in part as a playful allusion to the negotiations
for Anne's hand in marriage.[48]

A New Era

Even if *The Parliament of Fowls* was written (or read) for Richard
and his circle, it does not appear to have been commissioned or
patronized by the young king. Indeed, there is little evidence of
any form of literary patronage on Richard's part, despite the fact
that his court attracted such literary men as Chaucer, John
Clanvowe, Sir John Montagu and Gower, who dedicated his first
version of the *Confessio amantis* to Richard.[49] Nonetheless,
Richard's adulthood coincided with the production of a number
of major vernacular literary works, though this may have been
more connected with Richard's court circles than with the king
himself.[50]

Despite the unlikelihood that *The Parliament of Fowls* was
directly commissioned by the king, its charm and elegance reflect
something of the aesthetics of Richard's reign, visible today in

the artwork that survives from the period. The *Wilton Diptych*, now housed in the National Gallery in London, is one such example. The proposed dates for its creation range from 1377 to the final years of Richard's reign, to which it is now more commonly dated. The portable altarpiece consists of two painted panels of wood that depict Richard kneeling on the left, flanked by two English saints, Edmund and Edward the Confessor, as well as John the Baptist, whom Richard had adopted as his patron saint. These figures present the kneeling king to the figures on the right-hand panel: the Virgin Mary holding the Christ Child, who offers a blessing with his upraised hand. Surrounding Mary are eleven angels wearing Richard's personal badge, which featured a white hart. It is a powerful piece of propaganda, to be sure, but one that is undoubtedly visually pleasing. The Virgin Mary and the angels that surround her are draped in gowns of saturated blue, while behind them a golden diapered background glitters in vibrant contrast with the angels' softly feathered wings. Flowers are scattered across the grass beneath their feet. The king is no less splendid in a robe delicately painted over with fine gold strokes to mimic the texture of embroidery. Behind him and the three standing figures in the background, the sky is spangled with gold filigree shapes.

The *Wilton Diptych* is but one product of a reign that – despite the paucity of evidence concerning literary patronage – placed considerable emphasis on patronage of the arts. As Shakespeare's history play has now made famous, Richard was a king who was keenly aware of the importance of a powerful and refined royal image, and who took steps to cultivate that image through the commissioning of portraits and the purchase of gold, silver and jewels. Some sense of the extent of Richard's investment in the

Overleaf: unknown artist, *Richard II Presented to the Virgin and Child by His Patron St John the Baptist and Sts Edward and Edmund* (the *Wilton Diptych*), c. 1395–9, tempera on oak.

cultivation of a splendid public image can be gained from the fact that a manuscript roll in The National Archives that records an inventory of his treasure measures an incredible 28 metres (92 ft) long.[51]

The portrait of Richard II now known as the *Westminster Portrait* is further evidence of the king's agenda. The portrait is literally larger than life, and depicts Richard seated on a throne, a sceptre in one hand and an orb in the other. Staring directly at the viewer, Richard wears an expression that is at once stern and dispassionate, conveying his confidence in his right to govern. Such commissions and purchases reflect Richard's desire for absolute rule, with his splendid garments, jewels and portraits serving as a public display of power.

Though written roughly a decade before the *Wilton Diptych* and *Westminster Portrait* were likely completed, *The Parliament of Fowls* seems tailored for a courtly environment of lavish display. The dream setting is a garden of love into which the dreamer has been thrust by the famous political philosopher Scipio Africanus as a reward for the dreamer's literary labours:

> thus seyde he: 'Thow hast the so wel born
> In lokynge of myn olde book totorn,
> Of which Macrobie roughte nat a lyte,
> That sumdel of thy labour wolde I quyte.'

> thus he said, 'You have persevered so well
> By looking over my old torn book,
> About which Macrobius cared not a little,
> That I would like to reward you for your labour in some
> way.' (109–12)

The system of patronage in later medieval England was not unlike what Scipio describes here: a writer or artist would often

English school, *Richard II* (the *Westminster Portrait*), 1390s, oil on panel.

create a particular work with no guarantee of payment once it was completed. Instead, the work would be presented to a potential patron, who, if the work were pleasing enough, might then reward its creator in some way. With the various administrative, bureaucratic and diplomatic positions he held over the course of his lifetime, Chaucer would not have been fully dependent on such a precarious system, but it was one with which he would have been very familiar.

The Parliament of Fowls would also have been an appropriate poem for the courtly circles of Richard II because of its subject-matter, courtly love, one of the most fashionable topics of later medieval courtly poetry, having been popularized in the courts of medieval France. A highly stylized subject, courtly love might best be described as a loose set of ideals and expectations concerning male and female behaviour towards one another. Courtly love was distinguished by its idealization of the female object of a man's affection, as well as by its emphasis on excessive demonstrations of deference, fidelity and love through feats of bravery or generosity. Also connected to these stylized practices were demandes d'amour – that is, questions related to love, which members of a particular group or audience might be invited to debate among themselves. Was it worse, for example, to have an unfaithful lover or for one's lover to be dead?

The Parliament of Fowls presents readers with a demande d'amour debated among birds: when the three eagles begin to argue among themselves as to who should have the female eagle, the first claims that 'non loveth hire so wel as I [no one loves her as well as I do]' (435); the second claims that he loves her as well as the first eagle 'And lenger have served hire [and have served her longer]' (453); the third claims, 'I am hire treweste man/ As to my dom, and faynest wolde hire ese [I am her most loyal man, in my opinion, and the most eager to please her]' (479–80). Their argument ends in a three-way dilemma: which of the male eagles most deserves to have the female eagle? Failing to reach an agreement with one another, the participants in this debate eventually can do nothing more than quack and chirp in outrage.

The Parliament of Fowls playfully parodies the fashionable practices of courtly men and women by reducing those practices to chaotic cuckoos and quacks, but it does so within a framework that is elegant, charming and learned. Given Chaucer's contemporary reputation for comic writing, it is easy to focus on the silliness of the bickering birds rather than on the intricately constructed dream-frame within which they appear. But to do so would be to overlook the refined courtly culture on which Chaucer's poem draws, and for which it was written. Despite his physical and professional distance from the rarefied atmosphere of the royal household, Chaucer was more than capable of both appealing to and making fun of its fashions and practices.

* * *

In the early 1380s, Chaucer was entering a new phase of his poetic career. In poems like *The Parliament of Fowls* we see a more comfortable and confident use of humour to charm and amuse with gentle parody. The self-deprecation is still there – Chaucer is told that he will see something of love in his dream because he *isn't* a successful lover. But at this point in his career, Chaucer is mocking the person he has become: a low-ranking peripheral member of these courtly circles, someone who can jokingly claim to participate unsuccessfully in the discourses of courtly love instead of simply commenting on the love of others. At the same time, however, both Chaucer and his audiences also derived considerable amusement from a very different source: the well-established anti-feminist literary tradition.

Folio from *The Wife of Bath's Tale*, in a manuscript of Geoffrey Chaucer's *Canterbury Tales* (Ellesmere Chaucer), *c.* 1400–1410.

FIVE

Laughing at Women

bout halfway down folio 72 of the famous *Canterbury Tales* manuscript known as the Ellesmere Chaucer, a colourful image meets the eye. A woman sitting astride on horseback faces the column of text that appears on the left-hand side, brandishing a riding crop in her right hand. A broad black hat sits atop her kerchiefed head, framing a face that is ruddy-cheeked. The upper part of her garments is a brilliant red, her skirts a somewhat less brilliant blue and on her heel one can just make out the barbed shape of a spur.

This is the best-known portrait of Chaucer's most famous female pilgrim, and possibly his most famous character: Alison, the Wife of Bath, who was likely brought to life by Chaucer during what is believed to be the period in which he was working on *The Canterbury Tales* (from circa 1386 until his death in 1400). In many ways, the image that appears in the Ellesmere manuscript is relatively faithful to Chaucer's description of her in the *General Prologue*: her face is described as 'Boold', 'fair', and 'reed of hewe' ('bold, fair, and red of hue' (458)); she is 'Ywympled wel [wearing a large kerchief covering her hair and chin]' and wearing a hat that is 'As brood as is a bokeler or a targe [as broad as a buckler or shield]' (470–71). Perhaps the most notable detail for a medieval audience would have been the fact that on her feet she wears 'a paire of spores sharpe [a pair of sharp spurs]' (473), which indicates that, unlike most medieval women, she is riding astride. The spurs reflect Alison's desire for 'maistrie' (sovereignty), a desire that we also see reflected in her behaviour: she is loquacious and lively, and talks at great length – and in great detail – about her five marriages. When interrupted, she does not retreat into silence, but barrels ahead with her words. And, as her tale reveals, she believes that what women (or at least women like her) want most is *maistrie* – that is, sovereignty or the upper hand in marriage.

No wonder she's wearing spurs.

Alison may be a businesswoman whose clothmaking rivals that of Ypres and Ghent (448), but *The Wife of Bath's Prologue* makes it clear that what defines her is her status as a wife. She is

Miniature of the Wife of Bath, in the Ellesmere manuscript of Geoffrey Chaucer's *Canterbury Tales*, c. 1400–1410.

not simply someone who has married multiple times: she is a *fan* of marriage, and intends to 'bistowe the flour of al myn age/ In the actes and in fruyt of marriage [bestow the flower of all my age in the acts and fruit of marriage]' (113–14). And while the medieval Church taught that 'Virginitee is greet perfeccion' (105), Alison maintains that this lesson is meant only for those who wish to 'lyve parfitly [live perfectly]' – as she declares to her fellow pilgrims, 'by youre leve, that am nat I'.

Modern audiences tend to laugh along with the Wife of Bath, cheering her on as she points out the inconsistencies of the Church's teachings on marriage and virginity, celebrates sexual pleasure and challenges patriarchal *auctoritee*. Whether she is in conversation with her fellow pilgrims or in the bedroom, she takes no prisoners. But while modern readers might laugh in appreciation of Alison's outspoken nature, medieval audiences would more probably have laughed at what they viewed as the proof of her monstrous femininity: her vanity, her covetousness and her manipulation of her husbands. This was partly because Chaucer poached the very characteristics that modern readers tend to love from a literary tradition that was far from kind to women. Anti-feminist or misogynist texts had been written for centuries before Chaucer's lifetime, painting women as untrustworthy, vain and covetous harlots. These arguments were made both in earnest and in game, and shaped the experience of women Chaucer knew and interacted with, as well as his depictions of women in his writing.

If Chaucer's Wife of Bath has provoked various kinds of laughter over the centuries, some of the most important women in Chaucer's life have attracted the scorn, amusement or dismissal of contemporary scholars. This chapter explores the complex relationship between Chaucer's use of humour and his depictions of and references to women in his work, considering these alongside his relationships with two of the most important women in his life – his wife and his sister-in-law – as well as the much-debated accusation of *raptus* (usually translated as rape or abduction) long believed to have been made against him by a third woman, Cecily Chaumpaigne. As will become clear, not only do contemporary readings of Chaucer's literary depictions of women tend to be shaped by interpretations of his life-records, but inferences concerning the facts of his biography also tend to be shaped by views regarding Chaucer's writing and historical significance.

Better to Wed than to Burn

Chaucer's family connections and skills as a writer certainly helped him make a name for himself over the course of his career, but he was also helped by the family ties of his wife, Philippa. Born sometime around 1346, Philippa (known before her marriage as Philippa de Roet and possibly also as Philippa Pan) was the daughter of Sir Gilles de Roet (known as Paon), a knight of Hainault who had accompanied Edward III's consort, Queen Philippa, to England on the occasion of her marriage to the English king.[1] In contrast with Chaucer, who came from a mercantile background, Philippa was a knight's daughter, which put her and her sister, Katherine (later Katherine Swynford, the future mistress of John of Gaunt), a couple of rungs higher up on the social ladder.

Philippa likely met Chaucer when they were both working in the household of Elizabeth, Countess of Ulster. Chaucer's name is mentioned alongside that of a 'Philippe Pan' in the household's records of payments for 1357, when Chaucer might have been working as a page. When the countess died, Philippa went to work in the queen's household, and it may have been the queen herself who arranged for Philippa's marriage to Chaucer in 1366. Such an arrangement between household attendants was not uncommon, though it seems that household servants were usually discouraged from marrying one another.[2] 'Philippa Chaucer, one of the ladies of the chamber of Philippa, Queen of England', was granted an annuity of 10 marks by Edward III on 12 September 1366, which places the date of Geoffrey's marriage to Philippa on or before that day.[3]

We have no way of knowing what led Geoffrey and Philippa to marry, whether it was because of love or convenience or simply because – as the Church maintained – it was better to marry than to burn in hell for indulging one's lust out of wedlock. At the time they married and for several years thereafter, Geoffrey and Philippa continued to serve as attendants in royal households. This meant that they did not have much privacy, since most people in such a household were not given their own bedrooms or living spaces, whether they were servants, attendants or courtiers. Nevertheless, records suggest that within a few years of their marriage they had a son, Thomas (though his exact birth date is unknown), and they may already have had a daughter, Elizabeth.[4]

Despite the fact that Thomas was not the last child they would have during their marriage, Philippa and Geoffrey do not seem to have spent much of their life together under the same roof. There is no evidence that, when Chaucer moved to Aldgate in 1374, his wife and children accompanied him, and in later years Philippa followed her sister's household around the country while Geoffrey worked in London and travelled abroad. In 1386, for example, Philippa was with her sister in Lincolnshire, where she was admitted to the fraternity of Lincoln Cathedral on 19 February in a ceremony from which Geoffrey appears to have been absent.[5] She was in illustrious company: also admitted to the fraternity that day were Gaunt's eldest son, Henry Bolingbroke, Earl of Derby (the future Henry IV), Thomas Swynford (Katherine's legitimate son) and John Beaufort, Katherine's eldest son with Gaunt.[6] Though Chaucer's frequent

satirical remarks concerning marriage have led some to interpret
these periods of separation as evidence that his marriage with
Philippa was not a particularly loving one, it is also possible that
they were simply a pragmatic means of enabling Geoffrey to fulfil
his mounting administrative responsibilities and duties to the
Crown while Philippa helped the Chaucer family to maintain its
attachments to Gaunt and the royal household.

Critics have not always been terribly kind to Philippa Chaucer
over the years. Male critics have tended to read Chaucer's poetic
references to the 'wo that is in marriage [woe that is in marriage]'
(*Wife of Bath's Prologue* 3) as reflections of his own unhappy
marriage, in which he was hounded and nagged by a wife who
– they surmise – might even have provided inspiration for some
of the Wife of Bath's more unpleasant character traits. To put
it simply, these critics argue, 'To have depicted marriage as a
state of female domination and male disquiet, to have created a
character like the Wife of Bath . . . Chaucer must have had a
powerful experience of unnatural womanhood in his own life.'[7]

Philippa has generally been imagined as one of three 'types'
of woman: 'the plain, shrewish housewife; the promiscuous harlot;
[or] the independent "career woman"', none of which lines up
particularly well with either of the other two models of womanhood.[8] Even scholars who acknowledge the paucity of surviving
documentation pertaining to Philippa's life feel comfortable
suggesting that she might have considered Chaucer's career as
a controller to be beneath him.[9] But no matter how she has been
depicted by biographers and critics, Philippa has almost always
been presented as a potential obstacle to the realization of her
husband's literary genius – he succeeded *in spite of* her. Even the
alleged sexual assault of which Chaucer was long thought to
have been accused (discussed later in this chapter) has been at
least partially attributed to Philippa's occasional absences from
her London home on her travels to other parts of England.

While more recent biographies have included less of this sort of
wild speculation, they nonetheless suggest that Philippa's and
Chaucer's disparate ambitions may not have been compatible.[10]
The truth is that, outside of Chaucer's imaginative verse (which
lends itself to any number of interpretations), there is very little
evidence to suggest anything of the kind. Indeed, apart from
records of payments made and gifts given, very little documentary
evidence regarding Philippa's life and marriage exists.

Katherine Swynford

If Philippa's and Geoffrey's connections helped to put them in
a financially comfortable position, their situation was likely further improved when, not long after their marriage, John of
Gaunt began what would be a long-standing affair with Philippa's
sister, Katherine Swynford. When Katherine became Gaunt's mistress sometime in the early 1370s, the development 'unexpectedly
brought [Chaucer] into the orbit of greatness'.[11] Though Chaucer
was at that time serving in the royal household and might
already have written *The Book of the Duchess* in commemoration
of Gaunt's first wife's death, Katherine's new intimacy with Gaunt
meant that, by extension, Philippa and the Chaucer family
enjoyed a kind of vicarious new intimacy with the duke as well.

Like her sister Philippa, Katherine was accustomed to spending time among royalty and nobility, having been brought up
in the English royal court. From around 1365, Katherine worked
in the household of Blanche of Lancaster, Gaunt's first wife, where
her own daughter, Blanche Swynford, was raised alongside the
duchess's daughters, Philippa and Elizabeth.[12] Her husband, Sir
Hugh Swynford, was one of Gaunt's tenants, and fathered three
children with Katherine (Thomas, Blanche and Margaret) before
his death in 1371.[13] Upon the duchess Blanche's death in 1368,
Katherine became governess to Gaunt's children.[14] Her affair

with Gaunt may have begun as early as 1372, when he gifted
Katherine 'a generous sum of money'; their first son, John, was
born the following year.[15] In total, Katherine and Gaunt would
have four children together between 1373 and 1377.

Despite Gaunt's marriage to Constance of Castile in 1371,
his subsequent affair with Katherine appears to have been something of an open secret, one that provoked the ire of churchmen
such as Thomas Walsingham, who labelled Gaunt a 'fornicator
and adulterer'.[16] After Richard II's coronation in 1377, Gaunt
was even more open about his affair with Katherine, whom he
frequently visited at Kenilworth Castle, spending more time with
her than he did with his wife.[17] But as the example of Edward III's
despised mistress, Alice Perrers, makes clear, the mistresses of kings
and noblemen walked a difficult line. On the one hand, they and
their associates stood to benefit tremendously from their connections with royalty and nobility. On the other, should their affair
come to light or even be made deliberately public, they ran the
risk of being publicly condemned. Once Katherine's affair with
Gaunt became more widely known, an entry in the *Anonimalle
Chronicle*, for example, labelled Katherine a 'female devil and
enchantress'. As a consequence,

> in June 1381 Gaunt responded to the public mood that
> saw in the recent rising of the commons God's chastising of
> the sins of England's rulers by renouncing his relationship
> with Katherine and staging a reconciliation with his wife.
> Katherine gave up her post as governess . . . and retired
> from the Lancastrian household, with a further pension of
> 200 marks p.a., to live in some style at Kettlethorpe and
> Lincoln, where she rented a town house in Minster Yard.[18]

It is quite possible that the affair continued in a more discreet
fashion from that point forward until Katherine and Gaunt were

finally married in January 1396, after which their children were legitimized.

What Chaucer may have thought of his sister-in-law is impossible to know, although, as noted earlier, it has been suggested that a mocking reference to governesses in *The Physician's Tale* may be an example of Chaucer poking playful fun at Katherine. If this was indeed the case, it is worth noting what kind of joke Chaucer felt he could make at his sister-in-law's expense. The passage in question drily remarks that women were typically appointed as governesses either because they had successfully safeguarded their own virtue or, conversely, because their sexual experience rendered them familiar enough with 'the olde daunce' of courtship and seduction (79) to recognize when their charges were most at risk of losing their virginity. The latter suggestion draws on long-standing and widespread misogynist stereotypes of older women as sexually experienced tutors in the ways of love who could serve as agents for men seeking to seduce young women, one of the very same stereotypes that informed Chaucer's depiction of the lusty Wife of Bath.

Just as they do today, these sorts of misogynist stereotypes served to keep women in their place during the Middle Ages. Yet they were by no means a medieval invention: by Chaucer's lifetime, there already existed a well-established tradition of anti-feminist satire that stretched back at least as far as the Bible and the works of Aristotle. Many of the anti-feminist stereotypes that circulated then continue to circulate now.[19] Consider how familiar the following examples sound:

In the first place, women talk too much (and therefore cannot be trusted with secrets).
A woman marrying a wealthy man must be after his money.
Women nag their husbands.

Woman are less intelligent than men (but also tend to be
cunning).

Even when women pretend not to want sex, they want it
the most. (In the Middle Ages, women were widely
believed to be sexually insatiable.)

Statements like these may be found throughout medieval literature, in one form or another, proof that anti-feminist stereotypes
have changed very little over the centuries.

One of the most influential poems of the Middle Ages, the
satirical thirteenth-century French text *Le Roman de la rose*,
draws on many such stereotypes. The poem is a narrator's account
of an allegorical dream in which he fell in love with a rose and
was then hindered and helped by a variety of personifications
ranging from Shame and Gladness to Fair Welcome and even
Nature herself. Among the most memorable characters popu-
lating the dream is La Vieille, an old woman who, among other
things, imparts advice concerning how women ought to exploit
their admirers' affections. A woman, argues La Vieille, must get
everything she can from her lover in terms of wealth or jewels,
and make the most of her youth while it lasts:

She is a fool who does not pluck her lover down to the
last feather, for the better she can pluck the more she
will have, and she will be more highly valued when she
sells herself more dearly. Men scorn what they can get
for nothing; they don't value it at a single husk . . . Here
then are the proper ways to pluck men: get your servants,
the chambermaid, the nurse, your sister, even your
mother, if she is not too particular, to help in the task
and do all they can to get the lover to give them coats,
jackets, gloves, or mittens; like kites, they will plunder
whatever they can seize from him, so that he may in no

way escape from their hands before he has spent his last
penny . . . The prey is captured much sooner when it is
taken by several hands.[20]

Though *Le Roman de la rose* was popular and influential throughout the Middle Ages, some medieval readers argued that its
misogynist satire was potentially harmful to women, since it per-
petuated falsehoods that might lead men to abuse or otherwise
mistreat their wives. The poet Christine de Pizan (1364–c. 1430)
was among the most notable writers to object to the misogyny of

Bel Accueil looking at her reflection in the mirror while La Vieille
admires, miniature from a manuscript of the *Roman de la rose*,
c. 1490–1500.

Le Roman de la rose on these grounds; she took part in an epistolary debate regarding the supposed merits of the poem, a debate now referred to as the 'Debate of the Rose' (*Querelle de la rose*).

Le Roman de la rose not only influenced a great deal of Chaucer's writing but may have been translated by him into Middle English as well. In the prologue to the *Legend of Good Women*, the incensed God of Love berates Chaucer for having 'translated the Romaunce of the Rose,/ That is an heresye ayeins my lawe,/ And makest wise folk fro me withdraw [translated the *Romance of the Rose*, which is a heresy against my law and makes wise folk to withdraw from me]' (F Prologue 329–31). Four fragments of a Middle English translation of the *Roman* survive, though they cannot be linked to Chaucer with certainty. As penance for this crime against women and love, Alceste, the paragon of wifely virtue, commands Chaucer's narrator avatar to write 'a glorious legende/ Of goode wymmen, maydenes and wyves,/ That weren trewe in lovyng al hire lyves [a glorious legend of good women, maidens, and wives who were true in loving all their lives]' (F Prologue 483–5), women whose stories will serve as counterexamples of female virtue and fidelity. However, alongside such figures as Lucretia (a famously chaste Roman wife) and Philomela (a virgin raped and mutilated by her brother-in-law) are stories of women like Cleopatra (then best known for her seduction of Julius Caesar and Marc Antony) and, perhaps most surprisingly, Medea (who, among other things, murdered her own brother). Are these examples meant to be ironic? Are the narrator's profuse apologies for his (according to him) unintentionally anti-feminist poetry in the prologue insincere?

Questions like these might be asked of much of Chaucer's work. At several points in his poetry, Chaucer claims that it has never been his intention to slander or wound women. And it is true that his depictions of such characters as Criseyde and

Dido – whose stories elsewhere attracted censure or scorn – are remarkably nuanced and sympathetic in comparison with those of other medieval writers. And yet many of Chaucer's female characters behave in ways that are entirely consistent with anti-feminist stereotypes. In *The Miller's Tale*, Alison, the carpenter's wife, initially resists the clerk Nicholas's advances, but once she has given in to them seems to enjoy herself thoroughly, thereby casting doubt on the sincerity of her earlier protests. The character of the Wife of Bath is constructed out of the worst misogynist stereotypes about women. And even Criseyde, whose story Chaucer relays with such sensitivity in *Troilus and Criseyde*, eventually abandons her Trojan lover after she is forced to join her father in the Greek camp, a decision that for many medieval readers would have been difficult to view as anything less than further proof of women's lack of steadfastness in love.

It may seem astonishing that Chaucer could have felt so comfortable joking about his sister-in-law's mastery of 'the olde daunce' when her relationship with Gaunt was so advantageous to her relatives and associates, himself included. But such jokes were not uncommon, and reflected anti-feminist opinions that were widespread in the Middle Ages. In the prologue to *The Legend of Good Women*, Chaucer displays some awareness that these attitudes might not be appreciated by women themselves, a possibility that provides the fictional impetus for his writing of the *Legend*, and even for its presentation to a potential patron. Addressing the *Legend*'s narrator, Alceste commands, 'whan this book ys maad, yive it the quene,/ On my behalf, at Eltham or at Sheene [when this book is made, give it to the queen on my behalf, at Eltham or at Sheen]' (F Prologue 496– 7).[21] One wonders what sort of reception Chaucer expected his poem to have, particularly if the entire project of the collection of legends was ironic. Perhaps, in his eyes, hints of misogynist humour were not inappropriate in a work he hoped to present to the queen herself. But the question of how to interpret Chaucer's depiction of women and use of anti-feminist tropes was made still more complicated in 1873, when it was announced that documents had been uncovered that suggested Chaucer himself might have been accused of sexual assault.

De raptu meo

On 29 November 1873, *The Athenaeum* published a brief notice in its 'Literary Gossip' column concerning a recent discovery made by Frederick J. Furnivall and William Floyd in the Public Records Office: a document dated to 4 May 1380 in which a baker's daughter named Cecily Chaumpaigne released Chaucer from a charge of *raptus* ('de raptu meo').[22] As a later notice in *The Athenaeum* pointed out, the precise meaning of 'de raptu meo' in the document was unclear; since at least the end of the thirteenth century, *raptus* could be used to refer either to abduction or to sexual assault in legal records.[23] This ambiguity rendered 'the records of cases of rape virtually indistinguishable from cases of abduction' in later medieval legal documents.[24]

Despite the fact that the memorable word *raptus* is one reason why the Chaumpaigne case has received so much attention, scholars have been reluctant to mention 'either the noun *raptus* or "rape," its modern English translation; they have repeatedly tried to protect Chaucer's reputation from any association with so repugnant a crime as rape by simply avoiding that wrong's mention' and substituting any number of euphemisms in its place.[25] Conversely, more than one scholar has been tempted to fantasize about a pleasant encounter between Chaucer and 'a soft and pretty baker's daughter', effectively inserting the poet into a narrative that resembles the plot of one of his own *fabliaux*.[26] New documents that came to light after the initial 1873 discovery gave rise to various new hypotheses regarding what might have transpired between Chaucer and Chaumpaigne.[27] But the possibility that Chaucer might have been guilty of sexual assault remained a source of angst for contemporary scholars and readers of Chaucer's work for a century and a half.

In October 2022, it was announced that two new life records had been discovered in The National Archives. The documents in question suggest that, rather than being on opposing sides of a legal case concerning rape or abduction, Chaucer and Chaumpaigne were co-defendants in a labour dispute in which one Thomas Staundon had brought charges against them both under the Statute and Ordinance of Labourers.[28] The 1351 Statute of Labourers reinforced the 1349 Ordinance, and was a counter-measure against demands for better wages by labourers in the wake of the Black Death pandemic. Staundon claimed that Chaumpaigne had violated the statute by leaving his service 'before the end of the agreed term, without reasonable cause or license of Thomas himself, into the service of the said Geoffrey'.[29] The two scholars who made the discovery argued that in the context of this dispute, 'a radically different reading of *raptus* becomes possible', according to which Chaumpaigne's original quitclaim of 4 May 1380 was intended to *protect* Chaucer from any future charges connected with her 'physical transfer' from Staundon's household to Chaucer's.[30]

This discovery enables us to consider Chaucer's relationship with Chaumpaigne in an entirely new context, though it remains to be seen whether the proposed interpretation of *raptus* will be supported by surviving documents related to comparable cases. What other evidence makes much clearer is where things stood in relation to Chaucer's career at this point in time. By 1380, he was well established in his job at the custom house, though he had already been compelled to apply for permission to appoint a deputy on multiple occasions so that he might travel abroad on royal business. Chaucer's time was therefore divided between his living spaces over Aldgate, his working spaces in and around the port of London and occasional trips to the Continent. Of his personal life during this period, we know very little. The persistent scholarly interest in the Chaumpaigne case and the near-obsessive debate concerning the precise meaning of *raptus* are therefore all the more striking. They indicate the degree to which readers continue to be invested in salvaging Chaucer as a non-problematic figure within the English literary canon. Chaucer's popular image as a humourist further complicates matters – many readers want to be free to enjoy his work, despite its debts to the anti-feminist literary tradition and despite whatever crimes Chaucer may or may not have committed.

Laughing with Men

Whether or not Chaucer was teasing Katherine Swynford in *The Physician's Tale*, other poems suggest he was far from uncomfortable with anti-feminist humour. In fact, one of his surviving poetic *envoys* from the later years of his writing career, *Lenvoy de Chaucer a Bukton*, features a whole series of jokes concerning the supposed undesirability of marriage, jokes that Chaucer clearly anticipates his poem's male recipient will appreciate.

Bukton was likely written after Philippa Chaucer's death in 1387, and possibly as late as several years later, when Chaucer was at work on the composition and arrangement of *The Canterbury Tales*. By this point, Chaucer had been living away from London for some years, though the poem's addressee may have had connections with the royal court. *Bukton* is a relatively short poem, consisting of 32 lines distributed across four eight-line stanzas. It survives in only one manuscript: Oxford, Bodleian Library, MS Fairfax 16, in which Chaucer's poems appear alongside works by the fifteenth-century poets John Lydgate and

Thomas Hoccleve. The manuscript is probably a far cry from
how the poem's intended reader originally encountered it – a
poem like *Bukton* is more likely to have been circulated among
a very small group, though Chaucer may have read it aloud to
a private gathering at which its addressee was present.

Bukton is characterized by what one editor of Chaucer
describes as a slightly 'bantering tone', one that is simultaneously
teasing and self-deprecating.[31] Precisely which Bukton Chaucer
addresses in his poem is unknown, though it could be either a
Sir Peter Bukton from Yorkshire (the likelier candidate, in most
scholars' opinion) or the Sir Robert Bukton who was 'connected
with the royal court'.[32] The poem appears to be about Bukton's
impending nuptials, and contains a number of familiar anti-
feminist jokes about the woes of marriage, jokes that Chaucer
makes while repeatedly insisting that he intends to say nothing
critical of marriage. As he puts it,

> though I highte to expresse
> The sorwe and wo that is in mariage,
> I dar not writen of it no wikkednesse,
> Lest I myself falle eft in swich dotate.

> though I promised to describe
> The sorrow and woe that is in marriage,
> I dare not write anything disparaging about it
> In case I myself should relapse into such foolishness. (5–8)

Remarks such as these have led one scholar to describe *Bukton*
as 'an "occasional" poem, the occasion [being] a fourteenth-
century bachelor party', though of course this may not have been
the case.[33] Despite Chaucer's fervent declaration that 'I dare
not writen' and, later, 'I wol nat seyn [I will not say]' (9) anything disparaging about marriage, this is, of course, exactly what

Chaucer proceeds to do, comparing marriage to 'the cheyne/ Of Sathanas [the chain of Satan]' (9–10) and a type of 'prison' (14). Nevertheless, he echoes the well-known medieval justification for enduring the pains of marriage: 'Bet ys to wedde than brenne in worse wise' (18). That Chaucer wrote *Bukton* after Philippa's death is suggested by the fact that Chaucer refers to himself as no longer a married man: he writes as someone who claims to know from past experience just how awful marriage is, and who fears falling into that trap 'eft [again]' – once bitten, twice shy. The poem's final stanza urges Bukton to heed its advice. Should Bukton need further convincing, Chaucer writes, 'The Wyf of Bathe I pray yow that ye rede [I recommend that you read *The Wife of Bath*]' (29).

This last reference to the Wife of Bath is suggestive. After all, it is in the long prologue to her tale that Alison speaks extensively about her experience of marriage, which she claims grants her the authority to speak about its trials and tribulations. *Bukton*'s reference to the Wife of Bath indicates that by this point she existed in some form or other. She may already have been a character in a draft of *The Canterbury Tales*, or perhaps she was a character Chaucer was in the process of developing and discussing with his acquaintances. Whatever the case may have been, at this point in his career Chaucer was able to cite characters from his own work with some expectation that they might be known to others – the Wife of Bath was already taking on a life of her own. At the same time, it is a recommendation with a satirical purpose, the implication being that, if one really wants to know how awful marriage is (and, by extension, how awful women are), one need look no further than Alison herself.

Who Painted the Lion?

The early sixteenth-century Scottish writer Gavin Douglas famously described Chaucer as 'evir . . . all womanis frend [always all women's friend]'.[34] There are certainly several texts in which Chaucer claims to be a friend to women, or at least not to have defamed them. Near the conclusion of *Troilus and Criseyde*, for example, the narrator beseeches women not to be angry with him, excusing himself on the grounds that, while he was compelled to write of Criseyde's guilt, 'Ye may hire gilt in other bokes se [You may see her guilt in other books]' (Book v.1776). And enigmatic though his depiction of Criseyde might be, it is certainly much more charitable than Boccaccio's treatment of Criseida in *Il Filostrato*, the poem that was Chaucer's inspiration for *Troilus and Criseyde*. It is also true that *The Legend of Good Women* is framed as Chaucer's fictional penance for having slandered women in his poetry and translated *Le Roman de la rose*. But these protestations of innocence and hints of remorse are difficult to interpret because of a persistent tendency in Chaucer's writing about women and marriage: the tendency to take refuge in irony, disclaimers or apologies in the midst of texts that perpetuate anti-feminist stereotypes. The sardonic envoy at the conclusion of *The Clerk's Tale*, for example, addresses wives and entreats them never to imitate the meek and virtuous wife Griselda, who submitted to her husband's will without a word of complaint: 'Lat noon humylitee youre tonge naille,/ Ne lat no clerk have cause or dili-gence/ To write of yow a storie of swich mervaille/ As of Grisildis pacient and kynde [Let no humility nail your tongue down,/ and do not let any clerk have reason or make the effort/ to write a story about you of such marvel/ as the story of Griselda, patient and kind]' (1184–7). Other pilgrims, such as the Merchant, return to the theme of marriage's miseries: the Merchant opens his tale by declaring that 'We wedded men lyven in sorwe and care [we married men live in sorrow and misery]' (1228). If these are examples of Chaucer being a 'friend' to women, what need do women have of enemies?

There are many who have argued that the Wife of Bath is a kind of proto-feminist figure. But such arguments are difficult to support when the very qualities that make Alison such a vibrant and entertaining character to so many modern readers – her lively interest in sex and marriage, her desire to dress well and look good in public, her verbal domination of (most of) her husbands and even her misquoting of Scripture and patristic sources – can all be traced back to biblical, classical and medieval texts arguing against marriage and declaring the inferiority and infuriating nature of women.

And yet there are hints of a certain self-awareness on Chaucer's part, or at least an acknowledgement that stories are shaped by those who tell them. At one point in her prologue, the Wife of Bath notes that stories about women would read very differently had they been written by women themselves, instead of by men. She asks furiously, 'Who peyntede the leon, tel me who? [Who painted the lion, tell me who?]' (692). The question alludes to a fable in which a lion sees a painting of another lion being killed by a human hunter and points out that the painting would look very different if it had been painted by a lion instead of by a man. Alison's question turns a mirror onto the literary material out of which she has been constructed. It is a startling moment, a reminder that, after all, a man has painted this particular lion, using paints mixed by other men. And the very fact that Chaucer draws our attention to this is worth noticing.

* * *

Like the mixed picture of Chaucer's documented relationships and encounters with women, both the darkness and the humour of Chaucer's writing about women are two sides of the same coin. It is entirely possible that Chaucer enjoyed a happy (or at least useful) marriage at the same time as he wrote mockingly of the 'wo' of married life. It is possible that he was able to participate in the long tradition of anti-feminist satire at the same time as he took note of who was responsible for writing it. He may even have recognized that some forms of mirth came at a cost to the person being laughed at, rather than to the people doing the laughing. These apparently disparate aspects of Chaucer's life and work cannot and should not be separated from one another if we are to view him clearly. And if his ability to mingle self-deprecation, irony and mockery made his views on women difficult to discern, it would serve him well during one of the most turbulent episodes of medieval English history.

SIX

Conflict

O n 14 June 1381, a fourteen-year-old boy rode out to face an army of rebels at Mile End, so named because it lay a mile to the east of Aldgate. Though he was accompanied by a party of several noblemen, his short journey had not been uneventful: the group had already been mobbed after passing through Aldgate, prompting the boy's mother to flee back to the safety of the Tower of London. Upon his arrival at Mile End, the boy was met by a roiling crowd, some of whom waved flags and banners while others brandished heads on spikes.[1] But what none of those present could know was that this moment would be one of the key events in the most famous uprising of medieval English history, when a young Richard II rode out to meet the armed forces of the Peasants' Revolt.

By 1381, tensions in England were reaching boiling point. Since the middle of the fourteenth century, England had been shaken by turmoil that had been interspersed with brief periods during which disorder lay dormant, but always ready to rise to the surface at a moment's notice. Richard II's accession to the throne in 1377 at the tender age of ten years old initiated a period of political instability, as his uncle, John of Gaunt, and an ever-changing cast of family members, friends and councillors struggled to govern the realm and counsel the young king. And all the while, England continued to be embroiled in the series of conflicts with France now known as the Hundred Years' War.

In the summer of 1381, English social, economic and political tensions came to a head in the Peasants' Revolt, a large uprising that resulted in the deaths of more than 1,500 rebels. The years immediately following the uprising saw the increased persecution of so-called 'lollards': followers of John Wycliffe (c. 1320s–1384), a philosopher and priest who was highly critical of what he viewed as the corruption of the clergy, and whose teachings had influenced at least one of the leaders of the revolt, John Ball. At the very end of the fourteenth century, when Chaucer's own life was drawing to a close, the political clashes between Richard II and his critics would culminate in his cousin Henry's usurpation of the throne.

For most of England's population, the later fourteenth century was – to put it mildly – an interesting time to be alive. This was particularly the case for someone like Chaucer, who had long been connected to the royal court and to many of the major players in the drama of the century's closing decades. Under such circumstances, one might expect that a writer in his position would be inclined to take current events as a source of inspiration. But Chaucer's connections to these events, however slight, may in fact have prompted him to avoid addressing them in his writing.

Despite the fact that *The Canterbury Tales* features characters drawn from so many different corners of society, it is difficult to detect much social or political commentary of any kind in Chaucer's poetry, at least in comparison with the work of contemporaries such as William Langland, the alleged author of *Piers Plowman*. *Piers Plowman* is among the medieval English texts best known for their satirical treatment of both society and the monastic orders. In a series of dream visions, the poem's narrator, 'Will', encounters allegorical figures representing different 'estates' (particular groups within society) as he tries to learn how to live a good Christian life. *Piers Plowman* captures much of the social discontent of later fourteenth-century England (particularly with regard to the corruption of the clergy and those close to the king). The poem appeared in multiple versions, which Langland apparently revised over the course of his lifetime. It also inspired a number of imitations and was even referenced by the aforementioned rebel John Ball. In a letter to his comrades, Ball urged various allegorized figures to stand together in support of the uprising, and declared that another supporter of the revolt 'biddeth Peres Ploughman go to his werk' as it was time for social and religious reform.[2]

It is virtually impossible to identify anything like Langland's righteous indignation in Chaucer's writing. By contrast with the author of *Piers Plowman*, Chaucer seems strangely detached from even the most tumultuous events of his day, to which only a few sidelong allusions can be found in his works. Similar contrasts have been drawn between Chaucer and the author of the Arthurian text now known as *Sir Gawain and the Green Knight* (usually dated to the final quarter of the fourteenth century), with which Chaucer may have been acquainted. One scholar observes that, though texts like *The Parson's Tale* indicate that Chaucer 'was by no means indifferent to moral values', they were 'not usually his primary concern as they were those of the Gawain poet. Where Chaucer was humorous and detached, the latter was serious and engaged.'[3] Chaucer was clearly well acquainted with both the controversies of his day and the literary satire they inspired. His own ironic references to these controversies are not targeted attacks, however, but rather a more generalized mockery of certain well-known types. Perhaps this was a means of self-preservation for Chaucer during violently unstable times.

The Body Politic

In much of medieval Europe, social hierarchy was broken up
into different estates, usually roughly divided into the clergy, the
nobility and everyone else (primarily peasants and commoners).
This tripartite structure is illustrated in an illuminated initial
that can be found in a late thirteenth-century French manuscript
of the *Image du monde* (Image of the World) in the British Library.
On f. 85r of this manuscript, three figures are painted into the
space within a capital letter 'C': a cleric (representing *oratores*,
'those who pray'), a helmed knight (representing *bellatores*, 'those

The three estates: a tonsured cleric, a knight with a shield and a peasant
with a spade, miniature from a manuscript of Gautier de Metz, *L'Image
du monde*, 1265–70.

who fight') and a peasant (representing *laboratores*, 'those who work').[4]

Not every country in medieval Europe adopted precisely this social hierarchy. Later medieval English society eventually evolved into two estates, the first consisting of nobility and clergy and the second consisting of commoners (a structure that survives today in the division of the Houses of Parliament into the House of Lords and the House of Commons). But the same basic theory underlay all of these various social structures: everyone had their place within society, and everyone had to perform the duties of their position in order for society to function properly. This ensured the 'health', proper functioning and common good of the body politic as a whole. Failure to fulfil the duties of one's social position could lead to social collapse, political disaster and ruin. This view of the body politic placed different groups within the medieval English population in a position to judge and clash with one another if they felt that one or another of the groups was derelict in their social and political duties.

In the second half of the fourteenth century, pre-existing social tensions in England were exacerbated by the impact of the plague on the English population. While the bubonic plague did not discriminate between rich and poor, it decimated so much of England's working population that it led to a shortage of labour, which in turn prompted demands for higher wages. Resistance to providing those higher wages heightened tensions between the landowning classes and the working population, one of several factors that led to the Peasants' Revolt.

But there were other grievances as well, many of which were related to fears concerning Richard's youth and the perception that undesirable factions were exerting undue influence over him. Against the backdrop of more general social tensions, various political manoeuvrings were under way among members of the nobility hoping to gain control over the government. These manoeuvrings did not go unnoticed by either the general public or those who, like Chaucer, had the opportunity to observe them at closer range. While Gaunt had held the reins of power during the final years of his father's life, within a few months of Richard's ascension to the throne Gaunt felt obliged to publicly denounce those accusing him of coveting the crown. He declared his loyalty to the king before Parliament in the autumn of 1377. Despite this gesture, Gaunt was not among the nine councillors entrusted with making decisions on behalf of the young king. His role in the governing of the kingdom was much less prominent throughout the remainder of the fourteenth century, years marked by a series of clashes between Richard and Parliament.

Gaunt's general unpopularity was not improved by growing tensions between different factions in London, particularly between that of Mayor William Walworth on the one hand (mayor of London in 1374–5 and 1380–81) and that of John Northampton on the other. Walworth was allied with former mayors Sir Nicholas Brembre and John Philipot in 'opposition to the government-sold licences that allowed wool merchants to avoid paying tax', whereas Northampton was 'a maverick who promoted the interests of the vulnerable, and radicalised the allocation of power in the City. He wanted the poor to have a say in who represented them in Parliament and to end mercantile corruption.' Gaunt supported Northampton against Brembre, a member of the merchant elite whose power threatened to eclipse that of the Crown.[5] But Gaunt's actions and alliances made him even more unpopular with Londoners. On 13 June, one day before Richard confronted the rebels at Mile End, a group of rebels broke into Gaunt's magnificent Savoy Palace while he was away negotiating a truce with the Scots. They burned it to the ground.

A Tricky Position

By the summer of 1381, Chaucer had been in post at the Custom House for seven years. He was apparently still useful to the Crown, given his participation in royal marriage negotiations. His wife's sister was the mistress of the richest man in England, a man who might at any moment succeed in his quest to become king of Castile. All of this would seem to suggest that, at least on paper, Chaucer was in a comfortable position and could expect his life to continue that way.[6]

A closer look, however, suggests that Chaucer's position may have been rather more precarious than it appeared. His personal ties to Gaunt and his professional dealings with canny operators like Brembre put him between a rock and a hard place. Chaucer's initial appointment to the controllership placed him in 'a job that sat at the intersection of several urgently competing interests', a job that he never could have obtained if he had not met with the tacit or explicit approval of such parties as Brembre, William Walworth, the London wool men and the royal faction.[7] Moreover, even if the position carried with it a certain amount of social importance, it was not viewed favourably by most of the public. Partly because of their role in collecting duties and partly because they were suspected of corruption, 'Collectors and controllers were . . . universally mistrusted, resisted, and defamed': 'endless complaints about corruption, graft, cronyism, and lost revenue [were] registered again and again in Parliament'.[8]

Chaucer's residence in London may also have made him keenly aware of the dangers posed by the Peasants' Revolt. After all, the rebels had entered through Aldgate on their way into the City of London, directly beneath the rooms in which Chaucer was living. Chaucer may not have been home at the time this occurred, but it seems likely that he was in London: records show that on 24 May, a little over two weeks before the uprising, his annuity had been paid to him at the exchequer. A few weeks later, and less than a week after the rebels stormed into the City, in the London Court of Husting he quitclaimed his father's house in Vintry Ward, not far from where dozens of Flemings had been beheaded on the steps of St Martin's Church during the violence of the revolt.[9] That he found these events deeply unsettling is highly likely: not only was he associated with some of the chief targets of the rebels' ire, but he was himself 'one of the financial officials who might well have been a target for the rebels'.[10]

Apart from his renouncing of the house in Vintry Ward, the only other clue as to Chaucer's views on the Peasants' Revolt lies in a very brief reference to the event in his *Nun's Priest's Tale*, which is also the only sure reference to the revolt to be found in any of his works. In the tale, a rooster named Chauntecleer is carried off from the farmyard by a fox, which causes the other animals and a number of humans to give chase. Men and women, dogs, cows and geese yell 'as feendes doon in helle [as fiends do in hell]' (3389) as they pursue the fox and his prey:

> So hydous was the noyse – a, benedicitee! –
> Certes, he Jakke Straw and his meynee
> Ne made nevere shoutes half so shrille
> Whan that they wolden any Flemyng kille,
> As thilke day was maad upon the fox.

> So hideous was the noise – a, bless me! –
> Truly Jack Straw and his company
> Never made shouts half as shrill
> When they wanted to kill any Fleming
> As that same day was made about the fox.
> (*Nun's Priest's Tale* 3393–7)

However humorous the pursuit of the fox might be in the context of the tale, the scene depicted is one of chaos and imminent violence. Chaucer specifically compares the animals and humans chasing the fox with the rebels who burst into the City of London on 13 June 1381 and the next day dragged dozens of resident Flemings from a church to behead them in the street, leaving their corpses to rot. It is a jolting detail in the midst of an otherwise relatively charming animal fable, one that lowers the rebels to the level of animals and churls and reminds readers of how the rebels hunted their enemies through the streets of London.

Estates Satire

Chaucer's delicate position may partially explain why we do not find many direct or specific references to the well-known political controversies of the later fourteenth century in his verse. When it came to the vices and corruption of the Church, he was less reticent, but his anticlerical remarks do not stray far from mainstream critiques of the clergy. Throughout the later Middle Ages, monks, friars and other religious were widely believed to be more concerned with worldly matters and worldly pleasures than they ought to be. Consequently, at the time when Chaucer was writing, they were one of the most popular targets of a genre now known as estates satire.

Well before Chaucer's lifetime, classical and medieval writers had used satire to attack the various follies and abuses of the ages in which they lived. Popular targets frequently included political controversies, the corruption of the Church, different trends in fashion or fashionable behaviour and different groups within society (including women, as we have already seen). Chaucer was familiar with some of the most famous satirical texts of the classical and medieval periods, ranging from the works of Ovid and Juvenal through to Andreas Capellanus' De amore and the monumental Roman de la rose, both of which owed debts to their satirical predecessors. Despite the variety of their subjects and the contexts in which they were written, all of these texts use irony, exaggeration, sarcasm and other rhetorical devices for the purposes of ridicule and criticism.

Satire is not an especially merry mode of writing. Nevertheless, a satirical attack on a reviled target generates a certain kind of delight, satisfaction or even *Schadenfreude*, which is no doubt why there is such a long tradition of deriving entertainment from the ridicule and denunciation of others. Philosophers as ancient as Socrates, Plato and Aristotle are fairly united in 'allying humor with derision and ridicule', a link that Socrates attributes to the 'malice that makes us take pleasure in the misfortunes of others'.[11] In more contemporary philosophical discussions of humour, such views tend to fall under the umbrella of the 'superiority theory', which proposes that laughter originates in a sense of superiority over others, or over one's own former state.

The influence of estates satire is clear in much of Chaucer's writing. Medieval estates satire ridiculed the folly or vices of particular groups or 'estates' within society. The Middle English word *estat* refers to, among other things, 'a class of persons, esp. a social or political class or group; also, a member of a particular class or rank'.[12] Summarizing Ruth Mohl's definition of estates satire, Jill Mann writes that the genre is distinguished by four key characteristics (though she notes that they may not all appear in examples of estates satire, and that some elements of the genre may appear in other texts):

> First, an enumeration of the 'estates' or social and
> occupational classes, whose aim seems to be completeness.
> Secondly, a lament over the shortcomings of the estates;
> each fails in its duty to the rest. Thirdly, the philosophy of
> the divine ordination of the three principal estates [that is,
> the nobility, the clergy and the peasantry], the dependence

of the state on all three, and the necessity of being content
with one's station. And last, an attempt to find remedies,
religious or political, for the defects of estates.[13]

As has long been recognized, the pilgrim portraits of the
General Prologue to *The Canterbury Tales* owe much to estates
satire. At the most basic level, they capitalize on the tendency
of satire to lean into stereotypes: for all their individuality,
Chaucer's pilgrims are above all representations of specific types.
Few of them are given names, and all of them are presented in
terms of their station in life: a knight, a miller, a wife, a priest
and so on. Chaucer introduces them one by one, mingling indi-
vidualizing details with satirical stereotypes that would not have
been lost on later medieval audiences. Nearly every pilgrim is
described as an ideal example of his or her type, which implies
that they are also the most accurate examples of their respective
type's particular failings. Thus, the corrupt Pardoner (a licensed
seller of pardons and indulgences) sells items that he admittedly
knows to be worthless, but which he nevertheless claims may
help people secure salvation in the afterlife. The Manciple (an
individual responsible for purchasing food at an institution such
as a college or monastery) is forever on the lookout for ways to
cheat his masters.

   Social conflict is itself a key character in the frame narrative
of *The Canterbury Tales* – that is, the collection of prologues,
epilogues and exchanges between the pilgrims that take place
between (and even occasionally interrupt) the tales. The contemporary desire to think of Chaucer as a merry writer has led many
scholars to read these tensions and clashes in an optimistic light,
viewing them as signs of Chaucer's fictional depiction of a society capable of unity despite its internal squabbles. Marion
Turner, on the other hand, has argued that Chaucer's works
'present a vision of the social as fundamentally conflicted rather

than coherent'.[14] Particular conflicts repeatedly come to the fore
in Chaucer's works, and some of those may be linked to more
specific veins of medieval estates satire.

Estates satire was an especially apt genre with which to address
the upheaval of later medieval England and its social, political
and religious tensions. But Chaucer did not seek to capitalize on
this satirical potential in any particularly pointed way. This may
have been because of his own rather uncertain position – he may
not have thought it wise to risk angering the people who had
placed him in the controllership, the people who were his connections to the royal court or the people violently attacking
corrupt public figures by making others laugh at their expense.
However, he may have believed that he could easily find an audience for satirical writing about one group in particular: the clergy.

Anti-Fraternal Satire

If Chaucer was looking for one estate whose ridicule could unite
the largest possible audience in laughter, he would have found
the clergy to be a perfect target. That he clearly thought along
these lines is indicated by how frequently and deeply he mined
anticlerical satire for his portraits of characters such as the
Monk and Friar, as well as clerical characters in the stories of
The Canterbury Tales. If politics and social upheaval were major
sources of tension in later medieval England, so was the alleged
corruption of the Church and its clergy, an issue that intersected
with the socio-economic and political tensions that culminated
in the Peasants' Revolt.

Members of orders such as the Benedictines, Augustinians
and Franciscans were expected to adhere to vows of chastity and
poverty (among other things). But stereotypical depictions of
monks in anticlerical satire suggest that they were believed to
do quite the opposite: they were characterized by 'a love of good

food, luxurious clothing, a love of horses and hunting, contempt for patristic and monastic authority, laziness, a refusal to stay within cloister walls, [and] the temptations of holding various monastic offices'.[15] Many of these characteristics may be seen in Chaucer's depiction of the Monk in the *General Prologue* of *The Canterbury Tales*:

> An outridere, that lovede venerie,
> A manly man, to been an abbot able.
> Ful many a deyntee hors hadde he in stable,
> And whan he rood, men myghte his brydel heere
> Gynglen in a whistlynge wynd als cleere
> And eek as loude as dooth the chapel belle
> Ther as this lord was kepere of the celle.
> The reule of Seint Maure or of Seint Beneit –
> By cause that it was old and somdel streit
> This ilke Monk leet olde thynges pace,
> And heeld after the newe world the space.
> He yaf nat of that text a pulled hen,
> That seith that hunters ben nat hooly men,
> Ne that a monk, whan he is recchelees,
> Is likned til a fissh that is waterlees –
> This is to seyn, a monk out of his cloystre.
> But thilke text heeld he nat worth an oystre;
> And I seyde his opinion was good.
> What sholde he studie and make hymselven wood,
> Upon a book in cloystre alwey to poure,
> Or swynken with his handes, and laboure,
> As Austyn bit? How shal the world be served?
> Lat Austyn have his swynk to hym reserved!
> Therfore he was a prikasour aright:
> Grehoundes he hadde as swift as fowel in flight;
> Of prikyng and of huntyng for the hare

Was al his lust, for no cost wolde he spare.
I seigh his sleves purfiled at the hond
With grys, and that the fyneste of a lond;
And for to festne his hood under his chyn,
He hadde of gold ywroght a ful curious pyn;
A love-knotte in the gretter ende ther was.

A monk who rode out from the monastery on business,
    who loved hunting,
A virile man, worthy of being abbot.
He had very many fine horses in his stable,
And when he rode men might hear his bridle
Jingle in a whistling wind as clear
And also as loud as the chapel bell does
Where this lord was prior of the subordinate monastery.
The rule of Saint Maurus or of Saint Benedict –
Because it was old and somewhat strict
This same Monk let old things pass away
And followed the looser rules of modern times.
He did not give a plucked hen about that text,
That says that hunters are not holy men,
Nor that a monk, when he is heedless of rules,
Is like a fish out of water –
That is to say, a monk out of his cloister.
But he held that same text to be not worth an oyster;
And I said his opinion was good.
Why should he study and make himself crazy,
Always to pore over a book in the cloister,
Or work with his hands, and labour,
As Augustine commands? How shall the world be served?
Let Augustine keep his toil!
Therefore he was a vigorous horseman:
He had greyhounds as swift as a bird in flight;

Of tracking and of hunting for the hare
Was all his delight, by no means would he refrain from it.
I saw his sleeves lined at the hand
With fine squirrel fur, and that the finest in the land;
And to fasten his hood under his chin,
He had a very skillfully made pin of gold;
There was an elaborate knot in the larger end.
(165–97)

A lover of hunting and a despiser of manual labour, the Monk is described in terms of confidence and luxury. His appearance reflects his values and priorities: his girth is the result of fine dining and his 'bootes souple [supple boots]' and fine palfrey (a highly valued riding horse with a smooth gait) attest to his fine living. Even the items he compares to the tenets of his order – a plucked hen, an oyster – are comestibles, things he consumes.

While Chaucer's portrait of the Monk focuses on his enjoyment of worldly pursuits and consumption, his portrait of the Friar places more emphasis on his venal practices and lustful nature. Like the Monk, the Friar is a man who enjoys pleasure, but he is interested in a different pleasure of the flesh. Chaucer notes that the Friar 'hadde maad ful many a mariage/ Of yonge wommen at his owene cost [has made very many a marriage/ Of young women at his own cost]' (212–13), a detail that hints at the Friar's potential involvement with these young women prior to the marriages he arranged for them.[16] He is popular both with landowners and 'with worthy wommen of the toun' (217), and capable of sweet-talking a poor widow who 'hadde noght a sho [did not have a shoe]' (253) out of her last farthing. Most of the remainder of the portrait emphasizes the Friar's susceptibility to bribes and his preference for lively company in taverns rather than the beggars and lepers to whom he ought to be ministering: 'He knew the tavernes wel in every toun/ And everich hostiler and tappestere/ Bet than a lazar or a beggestere [He knew the taverns well in every town/ and every innkeeper and barmaid/ better than he knew a leper or a beggar-woman]' (240–42). The Friar prefers company that will help him 'profit', and such company does not include the poor or the ailing.

Chaucer resorts to anticlerical satire elsewhere in *The Canterbury Tales*, most notably in *The Summoner's Tale*. Recounted by a summoner (an official responsible for delivering court summonses to those accused of breaking Church law) as a come-back to the Friar's previous tale (which attacked summoners), the tale is preceded by a prologue that merges satire with scatological humour, inverting a thirteenth-century account of a vision in which the Virgin Mary shelters Cistercian monks under her cloak in heaven. The prologue describes how a friar descends to hell, but is reassured by the fact that, at first, he sees no friars there. He presumes this is because they are virtuous men, until the angel accompanying him urges Satan to lift up his tail, at which point swarms of friars fly out of the Devil's arsehole before return-ing whence they came. The tale that follows continues in this scatological vein, recounting the well-deserved misadventures of a greedy friar who is tricked by a man he is trying to wheedle money out of into accepting a 'donation' of a fart instead. Out-raged, the friar goes to the house of a noble benefactor and re-counts what has happened to him. The nobleman wonders how such a 'donation' might then be divided among the friar and his brethren (as was standard practice), until a squire offers a solu-tion: the friar's brethren should stand at the spokes of a wheel so that the fart can be evenly distributed among them from the centre, while the friar himself should stand at the centre in order to receive the fart directly.

The clergy were among the most popular targets of medi-eval satire, second perhaps only to women. We see a certain intersection of the two in Chaucer's portrait of the Prioress in

Miniature of the Prioress, in the Ellesmere manuscript of Geoffrey Chaucer's *Canterbury Tales*, c. 1400–1410.

The Canterbury Tales. Chaucer describes her as having some talents that might be expected of a medieval prioress (for example, the way the Prioress sings 'in hir nose' was recognized as a technique for easing 'vocal strain').[17] Other details, however, suggest not only that she is a little too worldly for a female religious but that she is overly concerned with how she appears to others. She fusses over her dogs, mimics courtly mannerisms and sports a shining golden brooch adorned with the phrase *Amor vincit omnia* (Love conquers all). The remark that, in the Prioress's behaviour, 'al was conscience and tendre herte [all was conscience and a tender heart]' (150) further suggests that, just as the Prioress is apt to 'countrefete cheere/ Of court' [counterfeit courtly manners]' (139–40), she carefully counterfeits an appearance of tender-hearted virtue. This hint at feminine deception infuses the portrait's anticlericalism with the flavour of anti-feminist satire. Readers who are invested in the idea of a 'likable' Chaucer may be tempted to imagine that the viciously antisemitic tale the Prioress goes on to tell – which simultaneously dehumanizes its Jewish characters and sentimentalizes the Christian child they martyr – was written as a satirical comment on her nature. But such antisemitism was typical of narratives and widespread attitudes in later medieval England, and there is 'no evidence . . . that the Tale was read, or could have been read, in Chaucer's own time as a satire on the Prioress'.[18]

* * *

In later centuries, Chaucer's anticlerical satire encouraged some to view him as a sort of proto-Protestant and chastiser of a corrupt clergy (John Foxe went so far as to suggest that Chaucer was 'a right Wicklevian', or Wycliffite).[19] John Dryden, writing of Chaucer's anticlerical satire in his preface to *Fables Ancient and Modern*, noted that 'A Satyrical Poet is the Check of the Laymen, on bad Priests.'[20] But Chaucer's trademark irony renders him a slippery character – his allegiances are difficult to discern with any real clarity. Might his emphasis on anticlerical satire – rather than the social and political satire of contemporaries like Langland – also have been a tool for survival in uncertain times? The clergy were certainly a relatively safe target for someone in his position; satirizing them for a late fourteenth-century audience was essentially preaching to the choir.

Chaucer's position at the margins of power in fourteenth-century England may have compelled him to become politically nimble in both his professional and literary work, ready to ally himself with whoever was in power at a given point in time. It may also have encouraged him to hone the irony that has come to rival his bawdy humour as one of the most distinguishing features of his poetry. But much like the words 'just kidding' after a particularly provocative joke, Chaucer's irony is also what makes it so difficult to know when one is supposed to laugh and when one isn't.

Though Chaucer himself was not directly implicated in many of the major conflicts of his day, he bore witness to them as someone who was closely connected to key players in these historic events, but whose professional and poetic work likely forced him to tread carefully. This would continue to be the case until the very end of his life and career. On 30 September 1399, Henry Bolingbroke was accepted as king; two weeks later, he was crowned Henry IV of England. When Chaucer wrote to Henry to appeal for payment of the annuity that had been terminated when Richard was deposed, he did so with apparent good humour in a short poem now known as 'The Complaint of Chaucer to His Purse'. In this mock love complaint, Chaucer simultaneously claims to address his 'purse' and the 'conquerour of Brutes Albyon,/ Which that by lyne and free eleccion/ Been verray king [conqueror of Brutus's Albion,/ which by line and free election/ is the true king]' (22–4). Chaucer addresses his purse as his 'lady dere' (2) and complains that she has been 'lyght' (3), a word that not only refers to the weight of his now-empty purse but suggests the wantonness and waywardness of his 'lady'. The first three stanzas of the poem conclude with a repeating refrain: 'Beth hevy ageyn, or elles mot I dye [Be heavy/pregnant again, or else I must die]' (7, 14, 21), playing with the double meaning of 'hevy' as either a reference to the weight of his purse or a reference to being with child. Claiming that he is 'shave as nye as any frere [shaved as closely as any friar]' (19), Chaucer comically stresses the urgency of his 'supplicacion' (26) to the new king.

The tone of Chaucer's 'Complaint' recalls the somewhat comical self-effacement with which he had once addressed

Henry IV's father in *The Book of the Duchess*. It also reflects Chaucer's pragmatic transferral of allegiance from one monarch to another (although, as the son of Chaucer's long-standing benefactor and eventual brother-in-law, Henry IV was more intimately tied to the poet than Richard II had been). The usurpation of the English throne was to be the last in a long series of upheavals that characterized Chaucer's lifetime. He navigated these cataclysmic events with some degree of success, and his 'Complaint' is further proof of how his self-deprecating humour could enable him to move in certain circles and reinforce particular connections. It is also an example of the playfully bawdy style that would come to be emblematic of his work for later readers.

A nun plucks penises off a phallus tree, marginalia from a manuscript of the *Roman de la rose*, 14th century.

SEVEN

Bawdy Chaucer

S hortly after a knight finishes telling an elegant classical tale to an audience of Canterbury-bound pilgrims, the group's discussion is rudely interrupted. A drunken miller named Robin shouts that he wants to 'quite the Knyghtes tale [repay the Knight's tale]' (3127) with a tale of his own. The innkeeper or 'Host' overseeing the tale-telling tries to persuade Robin to let 'Som bettre man . . . telle us first another [some better man first tell us another]' (3130). But in the end, the miller gets his way, and he tells a tale that is *very* different from the one the pilgrims have just heard.

This little scene serves as the transition between *The Knight's Tale* and *The Miller's Tale* in *The Canterbury Tales*. The Miller's interruption signals a significant change in tone and direction: in response to the Knight's Theban narrative of the love triangle between the noble Palamon, Arcite and Emelye, the Miller serves up a bawdy story featuring quite a different set of characters. In his tale, a clever clerk named Nicholas plots with a carpenter's wife named Alison to cuckold her husband, thereby disappointing a soppy clerk named Absolon (who has been trying – unsuccessfully – to woo Alison for himself for some time). Where *The Knight's Tale* had concluded with a climactic battle scene and sombre funeral rites, *The Miller's Tale* concludes with slapstick: Alison tricks Absolon into kissing her arse, which angers him into seeking revenge by means of a red-hot poker (though the arse he ends up scalding with it is in fact Nicholas's). All of this is framed as the Miller's way of 'quiting' – paying back – the Knight for his tale.

The Miller is not particularly hostile towards the Knight. But his interruption heightens our sense of what rivalries might underlie an otherwise innocent tale-telling competition. After all, while every one of the pilgrims is equally welcome – or, more accurately, equally compelled – to take part in the competition, they are far from being social equals. Just as notable is the Miller's change of genre: whereas the Knight's tale might be described as a classical romance, the Miller's is from the earthier medieval genre of *fabliau* – a short, comic tale featuring bawdy humour.

The Miller's tale has played an important role in determining how readers have conceived of Chaucer over the centuries. While he has been known as many things – a 'father' figure in English literary history, a refiner of the English language, a master of social satire – Chaucer's 'mirth' and in particular his bawdy humour have come to dominate his popular reputation in recent years. This chapter considers Chaucer's bawdy humour in the context of his personal and professional life between 1386 – the year believed to mark the beginning of his *Canterbury Tales* period – and his death in 1400. In 1386 Chaucer's literary work and personal circumstances underwent significant changes. Some of these changes can be linked to the social and political upheaval Chaucer had recently lived through, and likely whetted his interest in the *fabliau* genre.

While *fabliaux* typically feature characters from the lower classes, most were written for the entertainment of more aristocratic audiences. This combination of characteristics may have been particularly appealing to Chaucer and his more aristocratic readers in the wake of the Peasants' Revolt. Chaucer's *fabliaux* also mark the culmination of his various experimentations with humour, in particular his engagement with satire and his self-deprecating poetic persona. Taken together, these various factors contributed a great deal to the reputation Chaucer currently enjoys as the medieval English master of bawdy humour, which for him was not simply a means of providing entertainment, but also a means of playing with literary conventions and audience expectations.

Turning Points

After the Peasants' Revolt, discord bubbled beneath the surface of life in the City of London. Various guilds were competing for political dominance. A few months after the uprising, the draper John Northampton campaigned against victualling guilds upon his election as mayor of London. The grocer Nicholas Brembre reversed Northampton's legislation upon his own election to the mayoralty in 1383, the second of four times he would be elected or appointed to that office.[1] And yet, east London remained a bustling, raucous mercantile space. Its streets rang with the sounds of commerce and public spectacles such as those that divert Perkyn Revelour, the dissolute apprentice of *The Cook's Tale*:

> For whan ther any ridyng was in Chepe,
> Out of the shoppe thider wolde he lepe –
> Til that he hadde al the sighte yseyn,
> And daunced wel, he wolde nat come ayeyn –
> And gadered hym a meynee of his sort
> To hoppe and synge and maken swich disport.

> For when there was any procession in Cheapside,
> Out of the shop thither would he leap –
> Until he had seen all that sight

And danced well, he would not return –
And gathered himself a group of like-minded companions
To hop and sing and make merry in this way. (4377–82)

This passage offers a snapshot of a city in which the fanfare of a procession might draw less-than-responsible young workers from their shops to make merry in the streets. Perkyn's case suggests that, on occasion, these workers were themselves the spectacle: his debauchery sometimes lands him in trouble, with the result that he is sometimes led as a prisoner with music to Newgate Prison, which lay at the west end of Cheapside (4402).

In the years immediately following the Peasants' Revolt, Chaucer was still in his controllership and living in his rooms over Aldgate. Though he was approaching the midpoint of his literary career, most Londoners would have known him (if they knew him at all) as 'a practical functionary – a man with suspiciously good court connections and a compliant partner of Nicholas Brembre and other city connivers'.[2] But on 4 December 1386, a man named Adam Yardley was appointed Chaucer's successor as Controller of the Wool Custom and Subsidy. Ten days later, Henry Gisors was appointed to succeed Chaucer as Controller of the Petty Custom in the Port of London.[3] Chaucer's lodgings over Aldgate had been leased to someone else since early October.[4] After more than a decade of juggling his responsibilities at the Custom House, his duties to the Crown and his more private work as a poet, Chaucer left the busy spaces of London for Kent.

Chaucer's move to Kent in 1386 proved to be a turning point for him both personally and professionally. He was now an established administrator, occasional diplomat and experienced poet in his mid-forties. Until this point, he had been living in the city that was the beating heart of English commerce, rubbing elbows with and working on behalf of powerful people. We have records of him travelling abroad to assist with negotiations between England and France as late as 1381, but records of only two trips survive after that date: one from the summer of 1387, when Chaucer travelled to Calais in a company on the king's business ('in obsequium regis', literally 'in obedience to the king'), and one from May 1398, when Chaucer was granted royal protection for travel to various parts of England on the king's urgent business.[5] Geographically speaking, Chaucer's world appears to have been shrinking.

His personal life was also changing. Sometime in the middle of 1387, only a few months after Chaucer had moved to Kent, his wife died of unknown causes. The last record pertaining to Philippa's life is an Issue Roll entry from 18 June 1387 that notes the payment of her exchequer annuity of £3 6s 8d to Geoffrey.[6] Since the annuity was paid twice annually, it is presumed that she died sometime between June 1387 and what would have been her next payment in the autumn – Chaucer collected payments only for himself in November 1387.[7] Philippa was survived by her sister, Katherine, who had retired to Lincoln in 1381 but eventually married John of Gaunt in 1396, after which their offspring were made legitimate by papal bull. What had once been relatively strong Chaucer family connections to the royal court had dwindled to little more than a slender thread.

Chaucer's working life, on the other hand, was far from over. Having been associated with the Commission of the Peace for Kent since 1385, Chaucer was reappointed a Justice of the Peace on 28 June 1386.[8] Though no records have been found related to any case heard before Chaucer, he appears to have held this position until 1389, a date that coincides with his appointment as Clerk of the King's Works at Westminster, the Tower of London and other royal properties.[9] It was during this latter appointment that Chaucer was robbed by highwaymen in 1390 at Hatcham in Surrey. His assailants took his horse, some belongings and

£20 6*s* 8*d* of the king's money (although, fortunately for him, Chaucer was released from any responsibility to pay back the stolen amount).[10]

As these glimpses of Chaucer's middle age make clear, he was living a very different life away from London. His changed circumstances coincided with a change in his poetry. Sometime around 1386, he began work on the text that would come to be most closely associated with his name: *The Canterbury Tales*. Some of the texts that would eventually be incorporated into this collection of stories had already been written by this point, and were even being alluded to by Chaucer in his other work.[11] And while the collection's moralizing or edifying narratives are the ones that appear most frequently in the eighty-odd fifteenth-century manuscripts and fragments of *The Canterbury Tales* that survive today, it was another genre that would ultimately come to be known as distinctively 'Chaucerian'.

The Origins of *Fabliau* and Bawdy Humour in Medieval England

Of all the genres in which Chaucer wrote, the one with which he has been most persistently associated is *fabliau*. This comic genre traces its origins back to twelfth-century France and the works of *jongleurs*, or entertainers. While its popularity in this region peaked roughly a century before Chaucer first travelled there, in the middle of the fourteenth century Boccaccio experimented with the genre in his *Decameron*, providing Chaucer with not only a model on which to draw for his own compilation of tales but several examples of *fabliau* narratives as well.

Simply understood, *fabliaux* are short comic tales that are 'scurrilous and often scatological or obscene'.[12] They are usually set in the medieval present and simply told, and their characters are typically drawn from the middle or lower classes. Despite their ordinary, everyday settings, any realistic quality that *fabliaux* might appear to have is in fact a *trompe l'oeil*: the apparent simplicity of plot and of the characters who act it out is in fact a product of careful set-ups and exaggerated character traits that, like satire, often draw on social stereotypes. And though it was previously thought that the low humour of *fabliaux* was aimed at members of the lower ranks of society, the opposite seems to have been the case: medieval aristocracy enjoyed scurrilous jokes and bawdy humour just as much as their social inferiors did. Perhaps the clearest evidence of this is the twelfth-century jester known as 'Roland the Farter', who entertained King Henry II at court every Christmas by performing a 'leap, whistle and fart' ('saltum, sifletum et bumbulum').[13]

While *fabliau* characters often include gullible husbands and social climbers who are members of the lower classes, *fabliau* audiences were made up of more aristocratic members of society – hence the tendency of *fabliaux* to 'parody lower-class attempts to adopt courtly behaviour'.[14] One example of this is when, in *The Miller's Tale*, the clever clerk Nicholas courts the carpenter's wife Alison by delivering a short yet quasi-courtly speech at the very moment when he is grabbing her by the 'queynte':

> privily he caughte hire by the queynte,
> And seyde, 'Ywis, but if ich have my wille,
> For deerne love of thee, lemman, I spille.'
> And heeld hire harde by the haunchebones,
> And seyde, 'Lemman, love me al atones,
> Or I wol dyen, also God me save!'

> secretly he grabbed her by the cunt
> And said, 'Truly, unless I have my way,
> For secret love of thee, sweetheart, I die.'
> And held her hard by the buttocks,

And said, 'Sweetheart, love me immediately
Or I will die, so save me God!' (3276–81)

The juxtaposition of courtly tropes (for example, the male lover claiming he will die unless the object of his affection gives in to his suit) with Nicholas's crude, grabby behaviour simultaneously points to one of the underlying aims of courtly love discourse (consummation) and presents these uncourtly characters' deployment of that discourse in a satirical light. This juxtaposition also enables the Miller to 'quite' (repay) the Knight's courtly tale with a tale that echoes its structure and themes, but which is much lower in tone.

It is tempting to read passages such as these primarily as satirizing courtly ideals and mannerisms, hinting that courtly lovers are not all that different from randy clerks: they only want one thing. Certainly the fact that Chaucer includes characters from so many different walks of life in *The Canterbury Tales* has encouraged many to view him as a kind of genial man of the people, a progressive optimist ahead of his time.[15] But if we recall the royal and aristocratic associates Chaucer mingled with throughout his career, his non-specific use of estates satire and his scornful reference in passing to the violence of the Peasants' Revolt, it seems less likely that he would have been inclined to sneer at the very class on which so much of his own career had depended, or to sympathize with members of the lower classes seeking to challenge the authority of their social betters.

Fabliaux in England

Chaucer has often been credited with writing the first *fabliaux* in English. While it is true that at the time in which he was writing, such tales had largely fallen out of fashion on the Continent, and were virtually non-existent in Middle English writing, Chaucer was not the first English writer to dabble in the genre. A single late thirteenth-century poem now known as *Dame Sirith* is the earliest and only known *fabliau* in Middle English outside of Chaucer's works. The poem relates the story of a clerk named Wilekin, who is unsuccessful in his attempts to woo a merchant's wife named Margery, and therefore seeks the counsel of an older wise woman named Dame Sirith. The older woman feeds mustard and pepper to her dog in order to make its eyes water, and pays a visit to Margery, who is tricked into believing that the dog is Dame Sirith's daughter, transformed into an animal because she refused the love of a clerk and forever weeping over her transformation. Horrified that this might be her own fate if she continues to refuse Wilekin, Margery decides to give in to his suit while her husband is away. The trickery and illicit sex of the poem place it squarely in the *fabliau* genre, as does the rather horrifying (if imaginary) threat of physical transformation. A similar text dating from the same period, the *Interludium de clerico et puella* (Interlude of the Student and the Girl) is a secular play in the form of a dialogue. Only two scenes survive, the plot points of which seem to echo those of *Dame Sirith*: a student tries and fails to woo a young girl named Molly, and then seeks out an older woman known as Dame Eloise, promising to reward her well if she helps him woo Molly successfully. Dame Eloise takes umbrage and refuses, claiming she is a holy woman, at which point the text breaks off. Despite its incompleteness, the *Interludium* seems poised to develop into another narrative of sexual trickery in the style of *Dame Sirith*.

The scarcity of *fabliaux* among pre-Chaucerian medieval English texts does not mean that medieval English writers and audiences were unacquainted with bawdy humour. Nor was bawdy humour confined to the genre of *fabliau*. Bawdy scatological or sexual humour and imagery could be found in many areas of medieval life, some of them quite unexpected. Visitors to

Sheela-na-gig from the church of St Mary and St David, Kilpeck.
Male figure with penis in mouth, Church of the Holy Cross, Avening.

medieval English cathedrals and churches might have noticed
stone carvings of women displaying exaggeratedly large vulvas;
many of these images, known as *sheela-na-gigs*, survive today,
such as the stone figure outside the south side of Kilpeck Church
in Herefordshire. While debate continues as to what these images
were intended to represent (a pagan deity, a symbol of female
fertility or something else), they were not uncommon, and could
even be seen alongside carved images of male figures in a state
of arousal (or, in the case of the Holy Cross church, Avening,
in Gloucestershire, a male figure with his penis in his mouth).
The margins of medieval manuscripts are famous for including bawdy images of all kinds. Some of these images appear to
be reflections of or commentary on the textual content that
appears alongside, while others appear to be evidence of medieval limners' playful sense of humour. Bent-over male figures
are painted with trumpets protruding from their arseholes; men
and women are depicted in the midst of sexual encounters;
and various unfortunate figures are drawn encountering the

bonnacon, a mythical beast resembling a bull that was believed to blast excrement from its anus as a defence mechanism.

Bawdy humour and sexual and scatological content may also be found in dramatic texts surviving from the Middle Ages. Manuscripts of medieval English plays that survive from the fifteenth and sixteenth centuries hint at the kinds of performances Chaucer might have witnessed as a member of a late fourteenth-century audience. In morality plays (allegorical dramas usually depicting clashes between vices and virtues), devilish characters and representations of sin and vice deploy crude language and humour in their discussions of how best to lead mankind astray. Even surviving mystery plays (dramatic performances of Bible stories, usually funded and performed by members of particular 'mysteries' or guilds) include humour that verges on the bawdy. The 'Second Shepherd's Play' from the Wakefield Cycle or Towneley Plays, for example, opens with bawdy anti-feminist banter about the pains of marriage and the

Miniature of the legendary bonnacon, from the Northumberland Bestiary, c. 1250–60.

fortunes (or misfortunes) of any man possessed of more than one wife. Bawdy narratives can even be found in medieval sermons, where they were perhaps included to make preachers' lessons more memorable (and less likely to send parishioners to sleep).[16]

Just as *fabliaux* were not the only places one might encounter bawdy humour in later medieval England, neither are they the only Chaucerian works where bawdy humour may be found. Perhaps the best example of Chaucer's earlier experimentations with bawdy – or at least suggestive – style is the character of Pandarus in *Troilus and Criseyde*, the story of the ill-fated love affair between the Trojan prince Troilus and the young widow Criseyde. The affair is brought about through the machinations of Criseyde's comical and rather sleazy uncle Pandarus, from whose name *pander*, a word for a bawd or pimp, derives. Though *Troilus and Criseyde* was based on Boccaccio's *Il Filostrato* (datable to sometime around 1335–40), Chaucer's Pandarus is much more comical than Boccaccio's Pandaro in the way that he urges on both Troilus and Criseyde and even orchestrates the consummation of their love. Chaucer's Pandarus may well have inspired Shakespeare's bawdy depiction of the character in his play *Troilus and Cressida*. But it was for the bawdy humour of his *fabliaux* in particular that Chaucer would come to be most famous.

Chaucer's Favourite Genre?

It is unclear why Chaucer chose to experiment so much with the comic genre of *fabliau* near the end of his life, when his poetic abilities were at their peak. As a genre that frequently depicted the downfall or humiliation of overly ambitious or gullible members of the lower classes for aristocratic audiences, *fabliau* may have seemed to Chaucer like a way to further ingratiate himself with his social superiors. It may even have struck him as a means of adopting a position that was virtually adjacent to that of his royal and aristocratic associates, joining them in the mockery of those they thought beneath them, and by means of a once-fashionable Continental genre essentially designed for that purpose. At the same time, the nature of bawdy humour, and in particular its flirtation with the limits of the literary, may have posed a welcome challenge for his poetic skills.

While there is no way of knowing exactly when or in what order Chaucer first began to compose his *fabliaux*, they seem firmly attached to his *Canterbury Tales* period – that is, the years between about 1386 and Chaucer's death in 1400. Helen Cooper notes that the first three *fabliaux* of *The Canterbury Tales*, the tales of the Miller, Reeve and Cook, were clearly written not only around the same period but 'when Chaucer's poetic skill was at its most developed'.[17] They are also among the tales that circulated in the most consistent order, a pattern that suggests Chaucer had a very clear plan for the opening structure of *The Canterbury Tales*.

The cluster of *fabliaux* near the beginning of *The Canterbury Tales* also helps to establish a clear precedent and tone for the remaining prologues and tales, setting in motion a pattern of payback. *The Miller's Tale* 'quites' *The Knight's Tale*, but it also prompts the Reeve to 'quite' the Miller (whose tale had personally offended him) with a tale that recounts the humiliation of an uppity miller. The bawdy humour threatens to escalate with *The Cook's Tale* but cuts off abruptly just as it mentions that one character's landlady 'swyved' (screwed) for a living. It is possible that Chaucer abandoned the narrative as too obscene, or intended to finish it at a later date. Or perhaps he always intended for it to be cut off by other characters before it could reach what would almost certainly be an extremely obscene conclusion.[18]

The abrupt ending of *The Cook's Tale* is not the only mystery related to Chaucer's *fabliaux*. Clues elsewhere in the manuscripts of *The Canterbury Tales* suggest that Chaucer had not yet established which pilgrim would be responsible for telling certain bawdy narratives within the fictional framework of the *Tales*. Some manuscript variants, for example, suggest that *The Shipman's Tale*, concerning a crafty monk who outwits both his lover and her husband, might originally have been intended for a female narrator (perhaps the lively Wife of Bath). While the conflicting and incomplete evidence at our disposal makes it difficult to draw conclusions about Chaucer's intentions, the limits and possibilities of *fabliaux* seem to have held a strong fascination for him. Other texts such as *The Merchant's Tale* show Chaucer playing with *fabliau* elements in the context of other forms and styles. The tale recounts the lecherous old knight January's marriage to the young and pretty May, who eventually cuckolds him by having sex with his squire, Damyan, in a pear tree, an episode that upends the expectations and tropes of the romance genre. Chaucer's depiction of January's lust and May's desire to cavort with his young squire results in a bitterly satirical picture of marriage between an old man and a much younger bride. At one point the tale's anti-marriage narrator remarks sardonically, 'Whan tendre youthe hath wedded stoupyng age,/ Ther is swich myrthe that it may nat be written [When tender youth has married stooping age, there is such joy that it cannot be written down]' (1738–9). The bawdy sex-in-a-pear-tree scene that initiates the tale's conclusion provoked both censure and celebration among the scribes who copied it: some left it out entirely in their copies of the tale, while others expanded on the scene in graphic detail.[19]

Chaucer may have experimented with *fabliaux* while at the peak of his poetic powers, but he did so using tools and tropes that he had developed over the course of his literary career. One finds elements of social, anti-feminist and anti-fraternal satire in their plots. The socio-economic tensions of Chaucer's time emerge in the occasional clashes between the pilgrims, though they are generally confined to conflicts between types. Women are depicted as making their way in the world by any means necessary in *The Shipman's Tale* and *The Merchant's Tale*, as well as in the Wife of Bath's lengthy prologue. And, of course, behind all of these tales is Chaucer's apologetic, self-deprecating pilgrim avatar, whose expressions of embarrassment precede the narrative that has come to be most closely associated with Chaucer's skill as a bawdy humourist: *The Miller's Tale*.

The Miller's Tale is an intricately plotted story that holds up a sort of carnival mirror to the classical elegance of *The Knight's Tale*. In place of a love triangle between two Theban knights and an Amazonian princess (who initially wants nothing to do with either of her admirers), *The Miller's Tale* presents us with two clerks vying for the love of a carpenter's wife. Unlike the princess Emelye, who hopes to remain an unmarried virgin for the rest of her life, the carpenter's wife Alison is not only married but apparently willing to commit adultery with one of her admirers. And where *The Knight's Tale* had frequently mused on the nature of destiny, the Miller repeatedly warns that 'Men sholde nat knowe of Goddes pryvetee [men should not know of God's secrets]' (3454). The Miller's use of the word *pryvetee* serves as a playful pun that extends in multiple directions, from *privy* ('secret', but also 'toilet') to *privitee* (referring to genitalia). Taken together, *The Knight's Tale* and *The Miller's Tale* form a literary diptych that showcases Chaucer's range, poetic sophistication, mastery of plotting and comic touch to the full. By this point in his career, Chaucer was capable of adapting a classical narrative from a Continental source, but he was also able to use *fabliaux* to invert and poke fun at that same classical narrative.

Somewhat ironically, we see a hint of how much care Chaucer invests in his *fabliaux* at the very moment when he seems to be divesting himself of responsibility for them. At the point in *The Miller's Prologue* when it becomes clear that the Miller will be allowed to tell his tale after all, Chaucer's narrator entreats the audience not to hold him responsible for the 'harlotrie' (ribaldry) of that and the other *fabliaux* that follow:

> For Goddes love, demeth nat that I seye
> Of yvel entente, but for I moot reherce
> Hir tales alle, be they bettre or werse,
> Or elles falsen som of my mateere.
> And therfore, whoso list it nat yheere,
> Turne over the leef and chese another tale
> . . . Blameth nat me if that ye chese amys.

> For God's love, don't assume that I speak
> With evil intent, but only because I must rehearse
> All of their tales, be they better or worse,
> Or else misrepresent some of my material.
> And therefore, whoever prefers not to hear this,
> Turn over the leaf and choose another tale
> . . . Don't blame me if you choose badly.
> (3172–81)

There is much here that recalls the hesitation and self-depreca-tion of Chaucer's earlier narrators in texts such as *The Book of the Duchess* and *The Parliament of Fowls*. But the directive that Chaucer issues to his readers here is quite different in tone: *Turn the page if you don't like it and choose something else. Don't blame me if you read on and don't like what you see.* Whereas in earlier texts Chaucer had presented himself as deferring to his audi-ence's preferences and whims, here he makes his audience respon-sible for whether or not they enjoy his work. As with Chaucer's apologetic 'Retractions', this warning also serves as a label, a guide for those readers who might want to read precisely the sort of tale that Chaucer claims to be disowning.

The Miller's Prologue demonstrates the extent to which Chaucer had evolved as a poet by the time he began to concentrate on *The Canterbury Tales*. Read in the light of this passage, the apologetic modesty of his dreamer-narrators appears much more conventional, more typical of the expressions of modesty one finds in so many medieval texts. By contrast, the disclaimer of *The Miller's Prologue* is unafraid to hint at its own artificiality, its role in the framing of what follows: its tone shifts almost immediately from that of someone begging ('For Goddes love') for a specific audience response to that of someone *telling* the audience how to proceed. The other little trick this passage performs lies in its pretence that the literary world in which Chaucer and his audience are participating is one in which the 'harlotrie' of *fabliaux* has no place. Chaucer would have expected the traditionally more aristocratic audiences of *fabliaux* to be in on such a joke. With the manner of someone who seems to be aware that he is about to deliver some of the greatest punchlines of his career, Chaucer uses the disclaimer not to put audiences off, but to prime them to pay attention to the 'harlotrie' to come.

* * *

The degree to which Chaucer's contemporary reputation is bound up with his *fabliaux* raises questions. What drew Chaucer to this genre? Why did he experiment with it so often? Why is this such a memorable part of Chaucer's legacy (apart from the fact that the obscene tends to be memorable)?

While that last question is the starting point of the following, final chapter, the answer to the first two questions might lie at least in part in the storminess of Chaucer's times and the position from which he viewed it. Late fourteenth-century England was practically pulling itself apart, riven by political tensions, uncertainty, religious anxiety and outbursts of violence. The ruling and toiling classes were for all intents and purposes at war with one another, but ideological and economic fault lines were also pitting some members of the same class against one another. And while the motley cast of pilgrims that populate *The Canterbury Tales* have often been read as evidence of Chaucer's optimistic interest in diversity and of his hope for an end to such conflict, it is difficult to find concrete evidence of such optimism in the myriad conflicts depicted in that collection of prologues and tales.

The final years of Chaucer's life were not uneventful. In the years immediately preceding Chaucer's death, Richard II had been remarkably free from significant challenges to his power, despite his former skirmishes with Parliament. England was enjoying one of several brief periods of peace that punctuated the Hundred Years' War with France. This unusual stability enabled Richard to centre the activity of his court around art and culture rather than war in the final years of his reign, during which such works as the *Wilton Diptych* and the large *Westminster Portrait* of Richard were likely completed. However, his position was not as secure as it might have been. He was still childless, and nowhere near as wealthy as his uncle, John of Gaunt, whose son, Henry Bolingbroke, not only was a distant possible heir to the throne but had been among the Lords Appellant who in 1388 had pushed back against what they viewed as Richard's tyrannical rule.

It may have been Richard's sense of his own precariousness that led him to banish Henry from England in 1398 for a period of ten years following a quarrel between Henry and Thomas Mowbray, Duke of Norfolk and Earl of Nottingham (who was himself exiled for life). But upon Gaunt's death in February 1399, Richard made the rash decision to declare Henry exiled for life, and expropriated Henry's inheritance from Gaunt.[20] In defiance of Richard's actions, in late June 1399 Bolingbroke returned to England from France, where he had spent his exile up to that point. He claimed to be returning for the sole purpose of recovering the land and property that Richard had seized from him. But within a few months it became clear that his true objective was to lay claim to the throne itself. On 29 September 1399, Richard was compelled to give up the crown. He was formally deposed on 1 October, and Henry was crowned king twelve days later. By the end of February 1400, Richard was dead, possibly starved to death during his captivity in Pontefract Castle.

Precisely where Chaucer felt his loyalties should lie during this period of upheaval is unclear, but the deposition of one king and the accession of another does not seem to have done him any harm. As we have already seen, the tone of his 'Complaint . . . to His Purse', in which he requests payment from Henry IV, is playful rather than timorous. It is written in the impish voice of a poet who at that very moment may have been in the midst of his experimentations with the bawdy style of *fabliaux*. By this point, Chaucer was perhaps already in residence at what would be his final lodgings: a tenement in the garden of the Lady Chapel at Westminster Abbey, which was leased to him in December 1399.[21] His name does not appear in any documents after the summer of 1400, and the fact that he 'did not receive payments on the Michaelmas portion of his annuities' in the autumn suggests that he may already have died by this point in the year. Though the specific date of his death is unknown, the 'traditional' date of his death is 25 October 1400.[22]

Geoffrey Chaucer as a pilgrim, miniature from the Ellesmere manuscript of Chaucer's *Canterbury Tales*, c. 1400–1410.

EIGHT

Becoming Chaucerian

What does Chaucer mean for us today? If one were to judge solely by how his name is used in the publishing industry, the answer would be that he represents a very particular style of bawdy humour. While most readers (and even many undergraduates studying English literature) are unlikely to have read a word of Chaucer either in Middle English or in translation, his popular reputation is sufficiently established for publishers to cite either his name or the title of his most famous work in order to market certain books as entertainingly rude. Thus, one recently published collection of translations of Old French *fabliaux* is touted as 'Bawdier than *The Canterbury Tales*'.[1] The cover of Peter Ackroyd's 2009 book *The Canterbury Tales: A Retelling* declares that it 'captures the vigorous and bawdy spirit of Chaucer's original . . . by explicitly rendering [Chaucer's] naughty good humour' (in this case, largely by means of four-letter words).[2] Under such circumstances, it is hardly surprising that the author of a 2018 article on Chaucer in *The Guardian* opened by declaring, 'The thing that most people know about *The Canterbury Tales* is that it's full of good old-fashioned filth.'[3]

If in the centuries immediately following his death Chaucer was primarily known as English literature's point of origin, it is for his bawdy humour that he is best known today. This is the case even in scholarly circles: in a lecture delivered at the 2012 New Chaucer Society Congress, Anne Middleton observed that 'pungently indecorous' speech has long been a central feature of Chaucer's reputation.[4] George Shuffelton has gone so far as to suggest that obscenity has become the cornerstone of not only Chaucer's fame but his canonical status.[5] Chaucer's reputation for obscene humour has also bled into decidedly non-scholarly discourse: according to Urban Dictionary, the phrase 'to read some Chaucer' can be used as a euphemism for having sex.[6]

For better or worse, Chaucer's name has become synonymous with bawdy humour that is framed by disclaimers, tinged with irony and frequently attached to burlesque or satire. But how did this come about? This final chapter provides an overview of Chaucer's comic legacy and its shifting impact over the last six hundred years. While Chaucer's work has been reproduced and reappropriated in forms ranging from Robert Henryson's fifteenth-century Scottish addition to *Troilus and Criseyde* ('The Testament of Cresseid') to the pornographic *Ribald Tales of Canterbury* (1985), his protean use of humour has remained one of the most constant sources of inspiration for those who have sought to build on his literary legacy. At the same time, the fact that the writer so famous for his obscene comedy should also happen to be the so-called father of English poetry means that Chaucer's name and work are situated along an ever-shifting fault line between what is considered acceptable and what is considered unacceptable in works of art and literature.

Chaucerian Humour in the Fifteenth Century

As noted at the beginning of this book, after Chaucer's death 'mirth' was swiftly recognized as a cornerstone of his poetic legacy by some of his fifteenth-century imitators. In the prologue to his *Siege of Thebes*, Lydgate was among the first to draw explicit attention to the particular style of mirth found in *The Canterbury Tales* – namely 'ribaudye', the bawdy sort of humour featured in such tales as those told by 'the Cook, the Millere, and the Reve' (*Siege of Thebes* Prologue 25–9). Lydgate not only mentioned Chaucer's trademark ribaldry, he sought to imitate it with a rather clunky attempt at scatological humour later in the prologue, which inserts Lydgate's Theban narrative into the *Canterbury Tales* framework, with the Monk of Bury himself as an additional pilgrim.

In the prologue to Lydgate's *Siege of Thebes*, the Host (closely modelled on the innkeeper who oversees the *Canterbury Tales* tale-telling competition) addresses the narrator, who identifies himself as 'Lydgate,/ Monk of Bery, nygh fyfty yer of age [Lydgate, Monk of Bury, nearly fifty years of age]' (92–3). The Host then invites Lydgate to join their group and share a meal with them, observing that 'To ben a monk, sclender is youre koyse! [Your body is very slender for a monk!]' (102). The detail is a nod to Chaucer's satirical portrait of the well-fed Monk, as well as the Host's affected astonishment in *The Canterbury Tales* that a man like the Monk should be in religious orders.

Lydgate's Host then goes on to note that the poet-monk should take good care of his digestive system:

> Aftere soper slepe wil do non ille.
> Wrappe wel youre hede clothes rounde aboute.
> Strong notty ale wol mak you to route.
> Tak a pylow that ye lye not lowe;
> Yif nede be, spar not to blowe!
> To holde wynde, be myn opynyoun,
> Wil engendre collik passioun
> And make men to greven on her roppys,
> Whan thei han filled her mawes and her croppys.
> But toward nyght ete some fenel rede,
> Annys, comyn, or coriandre sede.

After supper, sleep will not do any ill.
Wrap your head with cloths all around.
Strong, nutty ale will make you snore.
Take a pillow so that you do not lie low.
And if it be necessary, don't hesitate to fart!
To hold gas in, in my opinion,
Will result in colic's passion [a sort of intestinal blockage]
And make men suffer in their guts
When they have filled their bellies and their gullets.
But nearer to night, eat some red fennel,
Aniseed, cumin or coriander seed. (108–18)

This passage is a peculiar combination of the sort of fart joke found in *The Miller's Tale* and Pertelote's advice to Chaunticleer to eat laxatives in order to avoid having bad dreams. The Host goes on to insist that Lydgate must be 'mery, whoso that sey nay [merry, no matter who objects]' (127), and that 'Yif eny myrth be founden in thy mawe [if any mirth may be found in your mouth]' (134), the Monk of Bury will be compelled to tell a tale just like the other pilgrims in the group. Lydgate here reinforces the image of *The Canterbury Tales* as a merry work, and of Chaucer himself as its merry author.

The ribald humour of *The Canterbury Tales* also inspired other fifteenth-century writers, including the anonymous author of what has become known as the 'Canterbury Interlude'. This spurious addition to *The Canterbury Tales* depicts the pilgrims' arrival in Canterbury, their visit to the shrine of St Thomas of Canterbury (Thomas Becket), their overnight stay and their departure. The text survives in only one manuscript datable to sometime around 1450–70, though the 'Interlude' is likely several decades older (dates proposed range from 1410 to 1420 or so).

As the twentieth-century editor of the 'Interlude' remarks, its author's familiarity with *The Canterbury Tales* seems to have been 'more intimate and wide-ranging than even Lydgate's'.[7] In addition to its lively depictions of the pilgrims themselves, the 'Interlude' includes a *fabliau*-like episode involving the Pardoner and a barmaid working at the inn where the pilgrims propose to spend the night. Like Lydgate, the author of the 'Interlude' opens by describing what kinds of tales the pilgrims have been telling on the road, particularly emphasizing those that were 'of other myrthes for hem that hold no store/ Of wisdom, ne of holynes, ne of chivalry,/ Nether of virtuouse matere, but to foly/ Leyd wit and lustes all [of other mirths for those who put no stock in wisdom, or holiness, or chivalry, nor in virtuous matter, but who applied their wit and desires to foolishness]' (4–7). This rather judgemental account of the sort of 'japes' ('trickery' (7)) that so often feature in *fabliaux* might seem like a prelude to an austere account of the pilgrims' arrival in Canterbury, but instead the text goes on to describe an encounter between the Pardoner and Kit, a 'tapster' or barmaid, that appears to be a set-up for a merry tale.

Kit welcomes the Pardoner 'with a frendly look, al redy for to kys [with a friendly look, all ready to kiss]' (23). While her readiness to kiss may simply be a matter of courtesy, the Pardoner grabs her around the waist 'As thoughe he had i-knowe hir al the rather yeer [as though he had known her all the previous year]' (26) and follows her into the taproom where her bed also happens to be. She explains that she lies there alone 'al nyght al naked' (28) because the man who was her lover is dead. The Pardoner expresses his sympathy for her situation. But it rapidly becomes clear that each of them is attempting to manipulate the other: 'etheres thought and tent was other to begile [either person's thought and intention was to beguile the other]' (126). The narrative bounces back and forth from these exchanges between Kit and the Pardoner to descriptions of what the other pilgrims are doing, with repeated remarks that both anticipate and delay each stage of the *fabliau*-esque plot. In the end, Kit manages to trick the Pardoner into giving her money for a delicious meal, which she consumes with others, rather than with him. She shuts the Pardoner out of her room, and when he whines outside the door, her lover (who was alive all along) shouts, 'Away, dogg, with evil deth! [Away, dog, with evil death!]' (483). When the furious Pardoner hurls insults at the barmaid, an extended knock-about scene ensues, at the end of which the battered Pardoner is forced to seek shelter with a dog that is not at all inclined to share its lodgings.

If the 'Canterbury Interlude' primarily features Chaucer's *fabliau* humour, a poem by the fifteenth-century Scots poet William Dunbar draws on both the bawdy and the anti-feminist humour of *The Canterbury Tales*. His satirical *Tretis of the Twa Mariit Wemen and the Wedo* (The Treatise of the Two Married Women and the Widow) tells of a male narrator who eavesdrops on three beautiful women gossiping about their husbands and lovers in a garden. The widow asks the two wives to reveal what bliss or misery they have experienced in marriage. The first wife responds with a description of her jealous older husband, whose beard scratches her whenever he embraces her (95, 105 ff.). The image recalls May's wedding night with January in *The Merchant's Tale* – the wife echoes May's sentiments when she exclaims that her husband 'may nought beit worth a bene in bed of my mystirs [he cannot satisfy my sexual needs worth a bean]' (128). After both wives have mocked and complained about their husbands, the widow speaks up and offers a kind of 'preching' (249) to the other two women. She explains how she took advantage of her own husbands while setting herself up to enjoy the company and generosity of many admirers once she was a widow. If the Wife of Bath is a lively and engaging character created out of many scraps of anti-feminist satire, Dunbar's widow is everything medieval misogynists feared and everything Chaucer warned Bukton against: a woman who maliciously exploits her husbands in order to ensure her own comfort and gain the freedom she needs to indulge her insatiable lust.

The Merry Father of English Poetry

In the middle of the sixteenth century, Chaucer's name came to be closely associated with ribald humour, a development that resulted in a bifurcation of opinion concerning Chaucer's legacy. On the one hand, he remained a foundational figure in English literary history and a model for English poets who came after him. He was also the first author in English to have his works collected in a single print volume when William Thynne published *The workes of Geffray Chaucer, newly printed*, in 1532. But on the other hand, Chaucer's *fabliaux* were coming to be viewed as a source of inspiration for sixteenth-century writers eager to write their own bawdy texts. At roughly the same time as Thynne's edition of Chaucer's *Workes* was first printed, Wynkyn de Worde published a short retelling of *The Reeve's Tale* titled *A mery iest of the mylner of Abyngton with his wyfe and his daughter, and two poore scholers of Cambridge*. Two distinct channels of Chaucerian publication were emerging: one that would eventually become the long tradition of serious editions and translations of Chaucer's work, and another that would develop into an equally long tradition of publications that celebrated and imitated his bawdy humour.

Various sixteenth-century references to Chaucer's 'mirth', 'japes' and 'jests' provide further evidence that he was well known for his obscene humour by this point in history. 'Chaucer's jest' became a term for intercourse, with the first such usage appearing in George Whetstone's 1578 play *Promos and Cassandra*.[8] A few years later, Chaucer's distinctive anatomical vocabulary led the authors of a 1585 medical dictionary to define the term *cunnus* as 'A woman's privy member called of Chaucer a quaint'.[9] Given such associations with Chaucer's name, it is no wonder that a playfully coy marginal note in the 1611 work known as *Coryat's Crudities* referred to the act of kissing a 'bomme' or backside as 'a Chaucerisme'.[10] Chaucer's name was becoming synonymous with jests, obscene humour and even female genitalia.

By the 1590s, this synonymity had made Chaucerian obscenity something that both invited critique and inspired explicit imitation. In 1590 an anonymous collection of stories titled *The Cobler of Caunterburie* was published. Like the stories of *The Canterbury Tales*, the *Cobler*'s tales are held together by a framing narrative about a group of story-swapping travellers (in this case, people travelling by barge from Billingsgate towards Canterbury). The titular Cobbler, a Smith, a Gentleman, a Scholar, a Summoner and an Old Wife each tell a tale in prose that is prefaced by a description in verse of the tale-teller in question. At the beginning of the *Cobler*'s frame narrative, the Cobbler expresses his admiration for Chaucer's *Canterbury Tales*, which he describes as 'pleasant to delight and witty to instruct'. He proposes that he and his fellow travellers imitate Chaucer's pilgrims by telling entertaining tales, which he even suggests they call 'Caunterburie tales'. But it soon becomes clear that the Cobbler and his companions have a very specific kind of Canterbury tale in mind: all but one of the tales in *The Cobler of Caunterburie* are centred on *fabliau*-esque scenarios involving cuckolded husbands, lovesick young men and cunning women.[11] Some of these stories enable the tale-tellers to spar with one another, recalling the squabbles and disputes between Chaucer's Canterbury pilgrims. For example, the first tale, told by the Cobbler, concerns a cuckolded smith, while the next tale, told by the Smith, concerns a cobbler who is cuckolded despite his jealous vigilance.

While the *Cobler* celebrates and imitates Chaucer's bawdy humour, other sixteenth-century texts suggest that some found Chaucer's bawdy humour objectionable. Criticism of Chaucerian obscenity appears in the prefatory remarks to Sir John Harington's translation of *Orlando Furioso*, published in 1591. Harington argues that it is absurd to criticize Ariosto for 'obscenousness' when Chaucer 'in both words & sence incurreth far more the reprehension of flat scurrilitie'.[12] By this point, Chaucer was so renowned for his bawdy humour that he could serve as a benchmark for what was (or ought to be) subject to criticism and censure. Some of those editing and publishing Chaucer's works felt compelled to address the issue of his ribaldry. Thomas Speght's 1598 edition of Chaucer's works is preceded by a letter by one Francis Beaumont that seeks to excuse and explain away those parts of Chaucer's verse that readers might dismiss or censure as 'filthie delightes'.[13]

It was not until the seventeenth century that the original Middle English versions of any of Chaucer's bawdier texts were published separately from the rest of *The Canterbury Tales*, and even then only in part. Richard Brathwait's 1665 *Comment upon the Two Tales of Our Ancient, Renovvned, and Ever-Living Poet Sr Jeffray Chaucer, Knight* (originally written sometime before 1617) presents extracts from the Middle English prologues and tales of the Miller and the Wife of Bath alongside Brathwait's paraphrases of and comments regarding the texts. Chaucer's Middle English text is printed in black-letter typeface, while Brathwait's words are printed in Roman typeface. That Brathwait is deliberately focusing on two of Chaucer's merrier works is suggested by the work's dedication page, which declares that the publication is 'primarily intended, & purposely published, for entertainment of retired hours'.[14] This statement foregrounds the entertainment value of Chaucer's works, rather than its historical importance or poetic significance. Likewise, the publication's focus on the Miller (who tells the first *fabliau*) and the Wife of Bath (whose description of her sex life is famously frank) suggests that, in Brathwait's view, Chaucer's capacity to amuse is specifically tied to the bawdy humour of *The Canterbury Tales*.

A later seventeenth-century publication further confirms Chaucer's reputation as an entertaining writer. In 1687 a collection of short, amusing (and occasionally bawdy) narratives was published as *Canterbury Tales: Composed for the Entertainment of all Ingenuous Young Men and Women at Their Merry Meetings*.[15] Attributed to 'Chaucer Junior', the collection is a compilation of stories set in Canterbury, including one based on the famous 'pear tree scene' in *The Merchant's Tale* and another that is a very truncated retelling of *The Miller's Tale*. Texts like these suggest that their authors expected readers to be familiar with Chaucer's reputation for merriment, and to associate his name with tales that resembled his *fabliaux*.

Avoiding 'Immodesty'

If the sixteenth and seventeenth centuries had witnessed the cementing of Chaucer's reputation as an entertainingly bawdy poet, the eighteenth century increased the rift between those who celebrated that reputation and those who saw it as a complication with which more serious readers of Chaucer had to contend. No single publication reflected this development more clearly than John Dryden's *Fables Ancient and Modern*, a compilation of translated excerpts from the works of authors such as Homer, Ovid, Boccaccio and Chaucer, whose Middle English excerpts are also included at the end of the volume.[16]

Fables Ancient and Modern marks an important series of firsts. It is the first time that any of Chaucer's *Canterbury Tales* were translated into modern English and presented alongside their original Middle English texts. It is also the first time that Chaucer was referred to as the 'father' of English poetry (although Thomas Hoccleve and other writers had identified Chaucer as a poetic father figure since the fifteenth century). But Dryden's remarks concerning Chaucer's 'ribaldry' also mark an important turning point in the transmission and reception of Chaucerian mirth. In his preface, Dryden explains, 'I have confin'd my Choice to such Tales of Chaucer, as savour nothing of Immodesty.' However, he also notes that, if he 'had desir'd more to please than to instruct', he would have included the more ribald tales of the Reeve, Miller, Shipman, Merchant and Summoner, 'and above all, the Wife of Bathe, in the Prologue to her Tale'.[17] Not unlike Chaucer's 'Retractions', Dryden's list of tales excluded from his *Fables* might also be read as a convenient list of tales some readers might be inclined to seek out *because of* their 'Immodesty'. It is also the first time that some of *The Canterbury Tales* are deliberately and explicitly excluded from a publication on the basis of their 'ribaldry' (even though Dryden acknowledges them to be entertaining).

In the decades following the publication of *Fables Ancient and Modern*, there was a profusion of different kinds of engagement with Chaucer's works, and with his bawdy humour in particular. For the first time in more than a century, a new edition of Chaucer's collected works was produced, though Thomas Urry's 1721 edition (published posthumously) is universally deemed to be of very poor quality. In 1775 Thomas Tyrwhitt produced a new edition of *The Canterbury Tales*, from which he expunged the 'superfluous ribaldry' that had been accidentally included in the work since Thynne's 1532 edition of Chaucer's *Workes*. The eighteenth century also gave rise to new adaptations of and responses to *The Canterbury Tales*, some of which expanded upon his bawdy humour. But in 1795 Chaucer's work was subjected to systematic censorship for the first time in William Lipscomb's publication of *The Canterbury Tales* 'in a modern version'.[18] While for the most part Chaucer's satire and anti-feminist humour were left untouched, his bawdy sexual and scatological humour was expurgated (including the entirety of *The Miller's Tale*). In his preface, Lipscomb attributes Chaucer's rude humour to 'the grossness and indelicacy of the times in which [he] lived', claiming that it was in fact because of his own 'veneration' for Chaucer that he, Lipscomb, had attempted to do Chaucer justice

> by purging him from his impurities, and by exhibiting him
> to a more refined age a safe as well as a brilliant example
> of native genius . . . It is hoped, as it is believed, that the
> pruning away of his indelicacies will not be found to have
> robbed him of any thing valuable, neither will the truth
> of the likeness appear to have been violated, since the
> exhibiting him free from stains has been effected
> scrupulously by the omission of the offensive passages,
> and not by the presumption to substitute fresh matter.[19]

Here, Lipscomb attempts a delicate balancing act, praising Chaucer's 'native genius' while striving to keep readers 'safe' from certain aspects of his work. This depiction of 'Chaucer's times' as utterly alien from the time of Lipscomb and his contemporaries is consistent with many eighteenth-century responses to Chaucer, which tended to offset praise for his literary achievements with remarks that his language was antiquated, his versification was uneven and his comic style was a reflection of the crude age in which he lived and wrote.[20] This was not the first time that Chaucer had been presented as both a product of and an exception to the tastes of his time (sixteenth-century writers had done precisely the same thing). It was also not the first time that a writer or editor thought certain readers should be shielded from Chaucer's ribaldry: where Dryden had simply decided to include only those tales that did not 'savour' of 'Immodesty', in 1718 Daniel Defoe had gone further, declaring that *The Canterbury Tales* were 'not fit for modest persons to read'.[21] But it was the first time that Chaucer's work had been explicitly presented as in need of censorship, and the first time such censorship had been carried out.

Children's Chaucer, Students' Chaucer

Just a few years after Lipscomb's modern version of *The Canterbury Tales* was published, none other than Lord Byron would declare that he found Chaucer 'obscene and contemptible'.[22] But over the course of the nineteenth century, Chaucer's *Canterbury Tales* would be cleaned up and made 'decent' for new groups of impressionable readers, including children.

The production of contemporary children's adaptations of Chaucer began with the 1833 publication of Charles Cowden Clarke's *Tales from Chaucer, in Prose*, although 'it was not until the 1870s, with [its] second edition (1870) and with Mrs. H. R. Haweis's *Chaucer for Children: A Golden Key* (1877) and Francis Storr and Hawes Turner's *Canterbury Chimes* (1878) that the fashion became established.'[23] In these early versions of Chaucer for young readers, the *fabliaux* do not seem to have been a natural fit; Steve Ellis remarks that 'it is obvious that discretion [had] to be exercised in the choice of [which *Canterbury Tales* to include]. In most compilations (with or without the "General Prologue"), one passes straight from "The Knight's Tale" to "The Man of Law's Tale," since the *fabliaux* are of course inadmissible.'[24] Instead of featuring Chaucer's naughtily humorous side, these early children's versions of his work emphasize 'romance, adventure, and fairy-tale elements' in their selected material (though *The Wife of Bath's Tale* appears in 80 per cent of children's adaptations of Chaucer's work, despite the rape with which it begins).[25] Overall, Chaucer is presented as a wholesome figure whose works can edify and delight innocent readers (Haweis includes 'a reassuring foreword addressed "To the Mother" in which Chaucer is held up as "a thoroughly religious poet"').[26]

The drive to produce wholesome, edifying and 'appropriate' versions of Chaucer for children during the nineteenth and early twentieth centuries coincided with the production of scholarly editions of Chaucer's works for a new generation of readers interested in approaching Chaucer as an object of serious study. The philologist and Chaucer enthusiast Frederick J. Furnivall was foremost among those who championed the works of the medieval poet. For Furnivall, Chaucer was not simply a titan of England's distant literary past, but someone whose works and style were worth knowing, either through the study of his Middle English text (perhaps with accompanying glosses in the margin or notes) or through translations and adaptations of his work. Furnivall and his contemporary Walter Skeat produced new editions of Chaucer's works, taking a fresh look at surviving manuscripts. In Furnivall's case, this enthusiasm for Chaucer's poetry was partly driven by his personal affection for the author, an affection inspired by Chaucer's wit and mirth.[27] His enthusiasm led him to found the Chaucer Society in 1868, which closed in 1912 and was ultimately succeeded by the New Chaucer Society in 1979. Organizations like these dedicated themselves to the study of Chaucer's life, times and works, and have shaped generations of teachers and scholars ever since.

By the middle of the twentieth century, Chaucer's bawdy humour was beginning to gain more universal acceptance, as much for its place in his work as for its supposed connections to his congenial, even laddish, persona. In the second half of the twentieth century, Chaucer's *fabliaux* and other bawdy writings came to be selected with greater frequency for student anthologies. Whereas John Manly's 1928 edition of *The Canterbury Tales* (whose intended audiences were primarily high school and undergraduate students) had 'omitted nearly all of the *Miller's Tale* on the grounds that "as a whole [it] is not fit to be read in a mixed company"', E. T. Donaldson included both *The Miller's*

Tale and *The Wife of Bath's Prologue* and *Tale* in the 1962 edition of the *Norton Anthology of English Literature*.[28]

Chaucerian Humour Now

In recent years, the bawdy humour of Chaucer's *Canterbury Tales* has come to the fore in the contemporary popular imagination. The idea that 'Chaucerian' can be understood to mean 'bawdy in an acceptably Old Englisshe way' has prompted new marketing tactics by publication houses, which tend to emphasize the 'naughty', 'bawdy' or 'rude' nature of Chaucer's *Canterbury Tales*. It has also directed the choices made by contemporary writers adapting his work. It is no accident, for example, that the pilgrim character on which Zadie Smith drew in her dramatization of part of Chaucer's work was the Wife of Bath, who might be said to embody the bawdy; and it is the Wife of Bath's colourful personal life, rather than her tale, on which Smith chooses to focus. The Kiln Theatre (at which Smith's play has been performed) notes that *The Wife of Willesden* focuses on the 'life story' of a woman named Alvita, and describes the play as a 'bawdy, beautiful comedy' that is also 'very, very personal'.[29] Its initial run at the theatre in 2021 sold out quickly, prompting a return in late 2022.

Chaucer's reputation for bawdy humour has a long history, one that continues to evolve. Entertaining though it may be, it is also something that deserves to be taken seriously, and to be considered in relation to not only the many other sides of Chaucer's 'mirth' but the social, ethical and moral concerns of his day. Like any other humourist, Chaucer invites readers to laugh at specific targets and with specific groups. His humour is written from a particular point of view. It can be easy to forget this, given how Chaucer's self-deprecating remarks and disclaimers paint him as an 'ironic', unassuming writer whose real position can never be divined from his words. And yet that ironic, unassuming quality is particularly striking in light of how much is often at stake. His jokes about women cloak and make light of the very real imbalances of power that shaped later medieval society. His pointed use of estates satire reflects the social suspicions and stereotypes of later medieval England. And it has become increasingly clear that many of Chaucer's self-deprecating remarks were written not only to conceal but to further his poetic ambitions. The fact that he so consistently provokes our laughter without engaging very deeply or directly with what is at stake in such laughter itself deserves our attention.

Just as ribaldry is not the only side to Chaucer's mirth, merriment is not the only side to his life and work. But reconsidering the events and experiences of Chaucer's life through the lens of his modern reputation as a genial, bawdy humourist reminds us of the original circumstances in which he was writing and the long-standing literary traditions on which he drew. Although writing poetry was only one part of how Chaucer spent his life, much was in the balance for him when he wrote it: not only political, social or professional survival, but his development as an English poet in a time when English poetry had yet to carve out a place for itself in the wider literary landscape of medieval Europe.

The things that Chaucer and his readers have typically found entertaining or 'mirthful' also remind us of what is at stake in laughter in our own time. The persistent fascination and discomfort provoked by his obscene humour offer us the opportunity to reflect on what we believe to be taboo in our own societies, and what we believe to be permissible in literature and other forms of art. The criticism that has enabled us to recognize the rape jokes at the heart of a *fabliau* like *The Reeve's Tale* can also help us see just how unacceptable such jokes are. In these respects, the life and works of the 'merry bard' continue to reveal both how much and how little has changed between Chaucer's time and our own.

CHRONOLOGY

1321	Death of Dante Alighieri
1327	Death of Edward II. Coronation of Edward III
1329	John Chaucer outlawed for participation in the uprising of Henry, Earl of Lancaster, against Queen Isabella and Roger Mortimer
c. 1330	Birth of John of Gower
c. 1335–40	Giovanni Boccaccio composes *Il Filostrato*
1337	Start of Hundred Years' War with France. Birth of Jean Froissart
1340	Birth of John of Gaunt
1341	Francesco Petrarca (Petrarch) crowned poet laureate in Rome
c. 1342	Birth of Geoffrey Chaucer
c. 1346	Birth of Eustache Deschamps. Birth of Philippa de Roet (later Chaucer's wife)
1348	Plague reaches England
1349	Document refers to John Chaucer's wife Agnes Chaucer, *née* Copton
1349–53	Giovanni Boccaccio writes the *Decameron*, which mentions the impact of the plague on Italy
1356	Battle of Poitiers
1357	First mention of Geoffrey Chaucer in the historical record, in household accounts of Elizabeth de Burgh, Countess of Ulster (which also mention 'Philippe Pan')
1359	Geoffrey Chaucer captured and ransomed during Edward III's military campaigns in France
1363	First Royal Charter of the Worshipful Company of Vintners
1364	Birth of Christine de Pizan
1366	Death of John Chaucer
c. 1366	Geoffrey Chaucer marries Philippa de Roet (possibly the 'Philippe Pan' mentioned in the Countess of Ulster's 1357 household accounts)
c. 1367	Birth of Chaucer's son Thomas
1368	Death of Blanche, John of Gaunt's first wife. Chaucer later writes *The Book of the Duchess* to commemorate her passing

1369	Death of Queen Philippa
c. 1370	Birth of John Lydgate
1371	John of Gaunt marries Constance (Costanza) of Castile
c. 1372	John of Gaunt begins affair with Katherine Swynford, sister of Philippa Chaucer
1372–3	Chaucer travels to Genoa and Florence
1372–85	Chaucer composes *The House of Fame, The Parliament of Fowls*
1374	Chaucer appointed controller of wool custom and subsidy and of the petty custom in the Port of London – he takes up residence above the gate of Aldgate. Death of Petrarch
1376	Death of Edward, the Black Prince. The Good Parliament
1377	Death of Edward III and coronation of Richard II. The Bad Parliament. Chaucer replaced at the great (wool) and petty custom by a deputy for the first time
1378	Chaucer accompanies Sir Edward de Berkeley to Lombardy on business relating to the war with France, grants power of attorney to Richard Forester and John Gower
c. 1380	Birth of Chaucer's son Lewis
1380	Cecily Chaumpaigne releases Chaucer from a charge of *raptus* ('de raptu meo')
1380–85	Chaucer composes *Troilus and Criseyde*
1381	Peasants' Revolt, after which Chaucer transfers the deed of his house in Vintry Ward to Henry Herbury
1382	Richard II marries Anne of Bohemia. John Churchman constructs a new Custom House in the Port of London
1384	Death of John Wycliffe
c. 1385	Chaucer begins work on the *Legend of Good Women*
1386	Philippa Chaucer admitted to the fraternity of Lincoln Cathedral. Chaucer permanently replaced as controller of the wool custom and subsidy and of the petty custom in the Port of London, gives up lodgings over Aldgate
c. 1386	Chaucer begins work on *The Canterbury Tales*
1387	Death of Philippa Chaucer
1389	Chaucer appointed Clerk of the King's Works
1390	Chaucer robbed by highwaymen in Kent
1394	Death of Anne of Bohemia, after which Richard II tears down Sheen Palace in his grief
1396	Katherine Swynford marries John of Gaunt, becoming his third wife
1398	Richard II banishes Henry Bolingbroke from England

1399	Death of John of Gaunt. Henry Bolingbroke seizes the throne from Richard II, becoming Henry IV. Richard dies within months. Chaucer takes up residence in a tenement in the garden of the Lady Chapel at Westminster Abbey
1400	Chaucer dies
1410–11	Thomas Hoccleve refers to Chaucer as a 'father' figure in his *Regiment of Princes*
1413	Death of Henry IV and coronation of Henry V
c. 1422	Birth of William Caxton

REFERENCES

Abbreviations

LGW   *The Legend of Good Women*
MED   *Middle English Dictionary*
STC   Alfred W. Pollard et al., *A short-title catalogue of books printed in England, Scotland, and Ireland and of English books printed abroad, 1475–1640*, 2nd edn (London, 1976–91) (later incorporated into the *English Short Title Catalogue*)
TEAMS Teaching Association for Medieval Studies

1 The Merry Bard

1 Cited in Derek Brewer, ed., *Chaucer: The Critical Heritage*, vol. 1: 1385–1837 (London, 1978), pp. 159–60.

2 Martin M. Crow and Clair C. Olson, eds, *Chaucer Life-Records* (Oxford, 1966), p. 525.

3 '[D]e malo et turpissimo amore hominum ad mulieres'; text and translation from Míceál Vaughan, 'Personal Politics and Thomas Gascoigne's Account of Chaucer's Death', *Medium Aevum*, LXXV/1 (2006), pp. 103–22 (p. 115).

4 '[V]e michi ve michi quia reuocare nec destruere iam potero illa . . . iam de homine in hominem continuabuntur Velim nolim'; ibid., p. 115.

5 Larry D. Benson et al., eds, *The Riverside Chaucer*, 3rd edn (Oxford, 2008), p. 328. All citations from Chaucer's works are taken from this edition. Translations of verse citations from *The Canterbury Tales* are adapted from those found on Harvard's Geoffrey Chaucer Website, https://chaucer.fas.harvard.edu/pages/text-and-translations, accessed 20 June 2023. All other translations of citations from his works are my own.

6 Regarding Chaucer's temperament, see John Dart's life of Chaucer in John Urry's posthumous 1721 edition of Chaucer's works, cited in Brewer, ed., *The Critical Heritage*, vol. 1, p. 182; Defoe's remark is on p. 174 of the same volume.

7 See, for example, David Mills, 'What Is Pinteresque?', *Sunday Times* (London), 5 September 1993, Features section.

8 Caroline M. Barron, 'Chaucer the Poet and Chaucer the Pilgrim', in *Historians on Chaucer: The 'General Prologue' to the Canterbury Tales*, ed. Stephen Rigby (Oxford, 2014), pp. 24–41 (p. 35).

9 Derek Pearsall, *The Life of Geoffrey Chaucer: A Critical Biography* (Oxford, 1992), p. 87.

10 On the tensions and interrelations between English and French cultural identities during this period and their impact on Chaucer's work, see Ardis Butterfield, *The Familiar Enemy: Chaucer, Language, and Nation in the Hundred Years War* (Oxford, 2009).

11 Ronald Waldron, 'Usk, Thomas (c. 1354–1388)', *Oxford Dictionary of National Biography*, www.oxforddnb.com, accessed 6 April 2022; L. C. Hector and Barbara F. Harvey, ed. and trans., *The Westminster Chronicle 1381–1394* (Oxford, 1982), p. 315 (original Latin on p. 314).

12 Pearsall, *The Life of Geoffrey Chaucer*, p. 96.

13 Peter Brown, 'Chaucer's Travels for the Court', in *The Oxford Handbook of Chaucer*, ed. Suzanne Conklin Akbari and James Simpson (Oxford, 2018), pp. 11–25 (pp. 11–12).

14 Brown, 'Chaucer's Travels', p. 12.

15 Ibid., p. 15.

16 Ibid.

17 Crow and Olson, eds, *Chaucer's Life-Records*, p. 535.

18 In *The Workes of our Antient and Lerned English Poet, Geffray Chaucer* (London, 1598), STC (2nd edn) 5079.

19 Thomas Hoccleve, *The Regiment of Princes*, ed. Charles R. Blyth, TEAMS (Kalamazoo, MI, 1999), l. 1961.

20 Almost nobody wrote poetry for a living in the later Middle Ages, unless they secured the support of a wealthy patron. Even then, the amount one was paid and the regularity with which one received payment were likely to be unpredictable.

21 Ardis Butterfield, 'Chaucer and the Idea of Englishness', *History Extra*, 24 December 2011, www.historyextra.com, accessed 28 March 2022.

22 John Lydgate, *The Siege of Thebes*, ed. Robert R. Edwards, TEAMS (Kalamazoo, MI, 2001), 'Prologus', l. 40 (hereafter cited above by line number).

23 Cambridge, Cambridge University Library MS Gg.4.27.

24 From Caxton's 'Prohemye' to his second edition of *The Canterbury Tales* (Westminster, c. 1483), STC (2nd edn) 5083, sig. aiiR.

25 Brewer, ed., *The Critical Heritage*, vol. I, p. 40.

26 Caxton, 'Prohemye', sig. aiiʀ.

27 Mills, 'What Is Pinteresque?'.

28 See Rosalind Field, '"Superfluous Ribaldry": Spurious Lines in the *Merchant's Tale*', *Chaucer Review*, xxvɪɪɪ/4 (1994), pp. 353–67.

29 Frederick Furnivall, 'Recent Work at Chaucer', *Macmillan's Magazine*, xxvɪɪ (March 1873), pp. 383–93, cited in Derek Brewer, ed., *Chaucer: The Critical Heritage*, vol. ɪɪ: *1837–1933* (London, 1978), pp. 167–77 (p. 174).

30 Marion Turner, *Chaucerian Conflict: Languages of Antagonism in Late Fourteenth-Century London* (Oxford, 2006), p. 2, here citing Stephanie Trigg's important study, *Congenial Souls: Reading Chaucer from Medieval to Postmodern* (Minneapolis, ᴍɴ, 2002), pp. xxi, 37.

2 Connections

1 See 'Introduction and Origins', www.vintnershall.co.uk, accessed 12 April 2022.

2 Douglas Gray, 'Chaucer, Geoffrey (*c.* 1340–1400)', in *Oxford Dictionary of National Biography*, www.oxforddnb.com, accessed 8 April 2022.

3 'Chaucer, Agnes', in *The Oxford Companion to Chaucer*, ed. Douglas Gray (Oxford, 2003), available online at www.oxfordreference.com, accessed 2 May 2022.

4 'Chaucer, John', in *The Oxford Companion to Chaucer*, ed. Gray.

5 'Chaucer, John', in Rosalyn Rossignol, *Critical Companion to Chaucer: A Literary Reference to His Life and Work* (New York, 2006), p. 371.

6 Marion Turner, *Chaucer: A European Life* (Princeton, ɴᴊ, 2019), p. 29.

7 Martin M. Crow and Clair C. Olson, eds, *Chaucer Life-Records* (Oxford, 1966), pp. 8–9 (deed transfer at pp. 1–2).

8 '[T]enementum cum domibus superedificatis solar[iis] celar[iis] ac . . . aliis pertinenciis'; ibid., p. 10.

9 See Glyn Coppack, *Medieval Merchant's House, Southampton* (London, 2003), pp. 4, 18.

10 '[I]n longitudine a vico regio de Thamystrete versus austrum usque ad aquam de Wallebroke versus aquilonem'; Thomas H. Bestul, 'Did Chaucer Live at 177 Upper Thames Street? The Chaucer Life-Records and the Site of Chaucer's London Home', *Chaucer Review*, xʟɪɪɪ/1 (2008), pp. 1–15 (p. 2).

11 Crow and Olson, eds, *Chaucer Life-Records*, pp. 8–9; Bestul,
   'Chaucer's London Home', pp. 6–7.

12 V. H. Galbraith, ed., *Anonimalle Chronicle, 1333 to 1381*
   (Manchester, 1927), pp. 145ff, cited in Erik Spindler, 'Flemings in
   the Peasants' Revolt, 1381', in *Contact and Exchange in Later Medieval
   Europe: Essays in Honor of Malcolm Vale*, ed. Hannah Skoda, Patrick
   Lantschner and R.L.J. Shaw (Woodbridge, 2012), pp. 59–78 (p. 62).

13 Bestul, 'Chaucer's London Home', p. 2.

14 Crow and Olson, eds, *Chaucer Life-Records*, p. 12; Turner, *Chaucer*,
   p. 38. See also Nicholas Orme, 'Childhood and Education', in
   Geoffrey Chaucer in Context, ed. Ian Johnson (Cambridge, 2019),
   pp. 219–29 (p. 219).

15 For more on the kind of education Chaucer likely received, see
   Turner, *Chaucer*, pp. 37–41.

16 Crow and Olson, eds, *Chaucer Life-Records*, p. 14.

17 The money is noted as having been given '[pro necessariis contra
   festu]m Nativitatis'; Crow and Olson, eds, *Chaucer Life-Records*,
   pp. 15–16.

18 Nicholas Orme, 'Childhood in Medieval England, *c.* 500–1500',
   www.representingchildhood.pitt.edu, accessed 3 May 2022.

19 Turner, *Chaucer*, pp. 44–5.

20 Crow and Olson, eds, *Chaucer Life-Records*, pp. 13, 16–17.

21 Lynn Staley, *Following Chaucer: Offices of the Active Life* (Ann
   Arbor, MI, 2020), p. 47.

22 *Stans Puer ad Mensam*, in *Codex Ashmole 61: A Compilation of
   Popular Middle English Verse*, ed. George Shuffelton, TEAMS
   (Kalamazoo, MI, 2008), l. 49, available online at https://d.lib.
   rochester.edu, accessed 27 April 2022.

23 Ibid., ll. 212–13.

24 Crow and Olson, eds, *Chaucer Life-Records*, pp. 19–20.

25 Staley, *Following Chaucer*, p. 47; see also Crow and Olson, eds,
   Chaucer Life-Records, pp. 94–122.

26 Turner, *Chaucer*, p. 79.

27 '[C]apto per inimicos in subsidium redempcionis sue'; Crow and
   Olson, eds, *Chaucer Life-Records*, p. 24.

28 Helen Carr, *The Red Prince: The Life of John of Gaunt, the Duke of
   Lancaster*, Kindle edn (London, 2021), p. 49.

29 London, British Library, MS Cotton Nero A.x/2, f. 128v.

30 William Shakespeare, *Richard II*, in *The Norton Shakespeare*, ed.
   Stephen Greenblatt et al., 2nd edn (New York, 2008), 2.1.65–6.

31 Ibid., 2.1.40.

32 See Carr, *The Red Prince*, especially Chapter Seven.

33 Ibid., p. 54.

34 Ibid., p. 60; Turner, *Chaucer*, p. 79.

35 Paul Strohm, *Chaucer's Tale: 1386 and the Road to Canterbury*, Kindle edn (New York, 2014), p. 29.

36 Monica H. Green, 'The Four Black Deaths', *American Historical Review*, cxxv/5 (2020), pp. 1601–31.

37 Ibid., pp. 1616–17.

38 Giovanni Boccaccio, *The Decameron*, trans. G. H. McWilliam, 2nd edn (London, 1995), p. 5.

39 Norman F. Cantor, *In the Wake of the Plague: The Black Death and the World It Made* (New York, 2001), p. 6; cited in Carr, *The Red Prince*, pp. 31–2.

40 See Helen Cooper's pair of essays ('Chaucerian Representation' and 'Chaucerian Poetics') in *New Readings of Chaucer's Poetry*, ed. Robert G. Benson and Susan J. Ridyard (Cambridge, 2003), pp. 7–50.

41 Larry D. Benson et al., eds, *The Riverside Chaucer*, 3rd edn (Oxford, 2008), p. 976.

42 The poem's French title is *La prière de Nostre Dame*, or *The Prayer of Our Lady*. See the note appended to the edition of the text found in *The Riverside Chaucer*, at p. 1076.

43 See *The Riverside Chaucer*, pp. 1060, 1065 (in the note pertaining to lines 496–7 of the F version of the poem's prologue).

3 Finding His Voice

1 James I. Wimsatt, 'Chaucer and the Poems of "Ch": Introduction', in *Chaucer and the Poems of 'Ch'*, TEAMS, ed. James I. Wimsatt, revd edn (Kalamazoo, MI, 2009), https://d.lib.rochester.edu, accessed 21 May 2022.

2 James Wimsatt, 'Chaucer and the Poems of "Ch": Introduction', notes that only four of the 'Ch' poems 'are chants royaux, and all of the lyrics in the manuscript are in some sense chansons'.

3 Ibid.

4 Michael Hanly, 'France', in *A New Companion to Chaucer*, ed. Peter Brown (Oxford, 2019), pp. 167–84 (p. 176).

5 David Wallace, 'Chaucer's Italian Inheritance', in *The Cambridge Companion to Chaucer*, ed. Piero Boitani and Jill Mann, 2nd edn (Cambridge, 2008), pp. 36–57 (p. 36).

6 On the languages of medieval English law, see Gwilym Dodd, 'Languages and Law in Late Medieval England: English, French, and

Latin', in *The Cambridge Companion to Medieval English Law and Literature*, ed. Candace Barrington and Sebastian Sobecki (Cambridge, 2019), pp. 17–29.

7 Hanly, 'France', p. 176.

8 Wallace, 'Chaucer's Italian Inheritance', p. 36.

9 Derek Brewer, ed., *Chaucer: The Critical Heritage*, vol. i: *1385–1837* (London, 1978), p. 40.

10 Ardis Butterfield, 'Chaucer's French Inheritance', in *The Cambridge Companion to Chaucer*, ed. Boitani and Mann, pp. 20–35 (p. 20).

11 See the passages and modern English translation from Froissart in Hanly, 'France', pp. 178–9.

12 Butterfield, 'Chaucer's French Inheritance', p. 27.

13 Anthony Bale, 'From Translator to Laureate: Imagining the Medieval Author', *Literature Compass*, v/5 (2008), pp. 918–34 (p. 921). See also Alastair Minnis, *Medieval Theory of Authorship: Scholastic Literary Attitudes in the Later Middle Ages*, 2nd edn (Philadelphia, PA, 2010).

14 Glending Olson, 'Making and Poetry in the Age of Chaucer', *Comparative Literature*, xxxi/3 (1979), pp. 272–90 (p. 274).

15 Albrecht Classen, 'Roads, Streets, Bridges, and Travelers', in *Handbook of Medieval Culture: Fundamental Aspects and Conditions of the European Middle Ages*, ed. Albrecht Classen, 3 vols (Berlin, 2015), vol. iii, pp. 1511–34 (p. 1521).

16 Ibid., p. 1524.

17 See Rodney Delasanta, 'The Horsemen of the *Canterbury Tales*', *Chaucer Review*, iii/1 (1968), pp. 29–36.

18 Martin M. Crow and Clair C. Olson, eds, *Chaucer Life-Records* (Oxford, 1966), pp. 477–89.

19 Romedio Schmitz-Esser, 'Travel and Exploration in the Middle Ages', in *Handbook of Medieval Culture*, ed. Classen, vol. iii, pp. 1680–704 (p. 1693).

20 *The Book of Margery Kempe*, TEAMS, ed. Lynn Staley (Kalamazoo, MI, 1996), Book ii, Chapters Six and Seven, https://d.lib.rochester.edu, accessed 21 September 2022.

21 Scott Lightsey, 'Chaucer's Return from Lombardy, the Shrine of St. Leonard at Hythe, and the "corseynt Leonard" in the *House of Fame*, Lines 112–18', *Chaucer Review*, lii/2 (2017), pp. 188–201 (p. 194).

22 Crow and Olson, eds, *Chaucer Life-Records*, pp. 53–61; Lightsey, 'Chaucer's Return', p. 190.

23 On the impact of the Black Death on labour legislation in medieval Europe, see Samuel Cohn, 'After the Black Death: Labour

Legislation and Attitudes towards Labour in Late-Medieval Western
Europe', *Economic History Review*, n.s., LX/3 (2007), pp. 457–85.

24 Helen Cooper, *Oxford Guides to Chaucer: The Canterbury Tales*,
2nd edn (Oxford, 1996), p. 50.

25 '[I]n secretis negociis domini regis', Crow and Olson, eds, *Chaucer
Life-Records*, p. 33.

26 Derek Brewer, *Chaucer and His World* (Cambridge, 1978),
pp. 100–101.

27 Derek Pearsall, *The Life of Geoffrey Chaucer: A Critical Biography*
(Oxford, 1992), p. 103.

28 Ibid., pp. 104–5.

29 Simon Horobin, *The Language of the Chaucer Tradition* (Cambridge,
2003), p. 36.

30 It is impossible to date the *Legend of Good Women* with any
degree of precision. Chaucer must have begun the prologue
to the poem sometime after Richard's marriage to Anne of
Bohemia in 1382, since she is mentioned in the earlier version
of the poem's prologue (F 496–7). And given that both versions
of the prologue mention *Troilus and Criseyde*, which was probably
written between 1380 and 1385 and certainly completed before
1388, Chaucer probably began work on the prologue sometime
in the mid- to late 1380s. Most scholars agree that the likeliest
explanation for her absence from the G version of the prologue is
that it was revised after her death in 1394. On the complications
of dating the *Legend of Good Women*, see Julia Boffey and A.S.G.
Edwards, 'The *Legend of Good Women*', in *The Cambridge
Companion to Chaucer*, ed. Boitani and Mann, pp. 112–26.

4 Custom and Craft

1 '[S]cutiferis camere regis', Martin M. Crow and Clair C. Olson, eds,
Chaucer Life-Records (Oxford, 1966), pp. 100–101.

2 Ibid., pp. 95, 98–100.

3 Derek Pearsall, *The Life of Geoffrey Chaucer: A Critical Biography*
(Oxford, 1992), p. 95.

4 Crow and Olson, eds, *Chaucer Life-Records*, p. 148.

5 '[E]n propre persone ou par suffisante depute pur qi vous vuilliez
respondre'; 'qe nostre seignur le roi eit damage ne perde
illoeqes et qe loial accompt eit rendrez et des issues des dites
custumes loialment respoundrez saunz fauxme ou fraude'; ibid.,
p. 158.

6 Paul Strohm, *Chaucer's Tale: 1386 and the Road to Canterbury*, Kindle edn (New York, 2014), pp. 90–91.

7 Jenna Mead, 'Chaucer and the Subject of Bureaucracy', *Exemplaria*, XIX/1 (2007), pp. 39–66 (p. 41).

8 In the summer of 2023 Richard Green claimed to have found a document written by Chaucer within The National Archives. See Dalya Alberge, 'Geoffrey Chaucer Note Asking for Time Off Work Identified as His Handwriting', *The Guardian*, 10 July 2023, www.theguardian.com.

9 Strohm, *Chaucer's Tale*, p. 97.

10 Mead, 'Chaucer and the Subject of Bureaucracy', p. 44.

11 '[A]d totam vitam eiusdem Galfridi'; Crow and Olson, eds, *Chaucer Life-Records*, p. 144.

12 Helen Carr, *The Red Prince: The Life of John of Gaunt, the Duke of Lancaster*, Kindle edn (London, 2021), p. 117.

13 Juliet Vale, 'Philippa [Philippa of Hainault] 1310x15?–1369', *Oxford Dictionary of National Biography*, www.oxforddnb.com, accessed 21 June 2022.

14 '[C]ynquante povre femmes esteantes entour le corps', and 'dousze povres hommes a tenir torches entour le corps'; Crow and Olson, eds, *Chaucer Life-Records*, pp. 98–100.

15 Carr, *The Red Prince*, p. 125.

16 Ibid., pp. 129–30; Nigel Saul, *Richard II* [1997] (New Haven, CT, 1999), p. 17.

17 The proverb is derived from Ecclesiastes 10:16: 'Woe to thee, O land, when thy king is a child' ('Vae tibi, terra, cujus rex puer est'). Douay–Rheims translation and Latin Vulgate, Ecclesiastes 10:16, www.drbo.org, accessed 4 March 2023.

18 Carr, *The Red Prince*, p. 131.

19 W. M. Ormrod, 'Edward III (1312–1377)', *Oxford Dictionary of National Biography*, www.oxforddnb.com, accessed 22 June 2022.

20 See the receipts and expenses from Chaucer's trips to Paris, Montreuil, and other parts of France between 17 February and 26 June 1377, in Crow and Olson, eds, *Chaucer Life-Records*, pp. 47–9.

21 Saul, *Richard II*, p. 24.

22 'Proceedings at the King's Coronation, 23 June 1377' (c 54/217 m. 45), online with transcription and translation at www.nationalarchives.gov.uk, accessed 18 July 2022.

23 Saul, *Richard II*, pp. 24–5.

24 Ibid., p. 26.

25 *The Westminster Chronicle*, pp. 414–15.

26 Ibid., pp. 416–17 n. 1. Richard presented the abbey with a replacement pair in 1390 (Saul, *Richard II*, p. 310).

27 Tim Tatton-Brown, 'Excavations at the Custom House Site, City of London, 1973', *Transactions of the London and Middlesex Archaeological Society*, 25 (1974), pp. 117–219 (pp. 121–2).

28 Ibid., p. 141.

29 Ibid.

30 Crow and Olson, eds, *Chaucer Life-Records*, pp. 170–76.

31 Ibid., p. 158.

32 Pearsall, *The Life of Geoffrey Chaucer*, p. 95; Crow and Olson, eds, *Chaucer Life-Records*, pp. 112–13.

33 Crow and Olson, eds, *Chaucer Life-Records*, p. 162–3.

34 '[A]d partes exteras in negociis regis profecturus'; ibid., p. 164.

35 Ibid., p. 165.

36 '[P]ur ascunes busoignes touchantes lexploit de nostre guerre'; ibid., p. 54.

37 Ibid., p. 54.

38 Ibid., p. 49.

39 '[P]ro certis negociis'; ibid., pp. 166–7.

40 '[P]ro quibusdam urgentibus negociis'; ibid., pp. 167–8.

41 James I. Wimsatt, '"Anelida and Arcite": A Narrative of Complaint and Comfort', *Chaucer Review*, v/1 (1970), pp. 1–8 (p. 1).

42 *The Riverside Chaucer*, p. 375.

43 A. Wigfall Green, 'Meter and Rhyme in Chaucer's "Anelida and Arcite"', *Studies in English*, II (1961), pp. 55–63 (p. 63).

44 Larry D. Benson et al., eds, *The Riverside Chaucer*, 3rd edn (Oxford, 2008), p. 383.

45 Crow and Olson, eds, *Chaucer Life-Records*, pp. 49–53.

46 Ibid., p. 50.

47 Pearsall, *The Life of Geoffrey Chaucer*, p. 127.

48 For more on the likely occasion for which *The Parliament of Fowls* was written, see Larry D. Benson, 'The Occasion of *The Parliament of Fowls*', in *The Wisdom of Poetry: Essays in Early English Literature in Honor of Morton W. Bloomfield*, ed. Larry D. Benson and Siegfried Wenzel (Kalamazoo, MI, 1982), pp. 123–44.

49 See Michael J. Bennett, 'The Court of Richard II and the Promotion of Literature', in *Chaucer's England: Literature in Historical Context*, ed. Barbara Hanawalt (Minneapolis, MN, 1992), pp. 3–20.

50 Saul, *Richard II*, pp. 360, 362.

51 Philip Lindley, 'Review of Jenny Stratford, *Richard II and the Royal English Treasure* (Cambridge, 2012)', *Speculum*, XCI/4 (2016),

pp. 1169–70 (p. 1169). The roll in question is National Archives
PRO E/101/411/9, which consists of forty membranes.

5 Laughing at Women

1 Marion Turner, *Chaucer: A European Life* (Princeton, NJ, 2019),
  p. 101.
2 Kate Mertes, *The English Noble Household, 1250–1600: Good
  Governance and Politic Rule* (Oxford, 1988), p. 180, cited ibid., p. 53.
3 'Philippa Chaucer, una domicellarum camere Philippe regine
  Anglie'; Martin M. Crow and Clair C. Olson, eds, *Chaucer Life-
  Records* (Oxford, 1966), pp. 67–8.
4 Turner, *Chaucer*, p. 118 n. 86.
5 Derek Pearsall, *The Life of Geoffrey Chaucer: A Critical Biography*
  (Oxford, 1992), p. 141.
6 Crow and Olson, eds, *Chaucer Life-Records*, pp. 91–2; Pearsall,
  The Life of Geoffrey Chaucer, p. 141.
7 Samantha Katz Seal, 'Chaucer's Other *Wyf*: Philippa Chaucer, the
  Critics, and the English Canon', *Chaucer Review*, LIV/3 (2019), pp.
  270–91 (p. 272). For records relating to Chaucer's possible daughter
  Elizabeth, see Crow and Olson, eds, *Chaucer Life-Records*, pp. 545–6.
8 Seal, 'Chaucer's Other *Wyf*', 273.
9 Pearsall, *The Life of Geoffrey Chaucer*, p. 128.
10 Ibid., p. 288.
11 Jane Griffiths, 'Biography', in *A New Companion to Chaucer*,
  ed. Peter Brown (Hoboken, NJ, 2019), pp. 38–49 (p. 38).
12 Helen Carr, *The Red Prince: The Life of John of Gaunt, the Duke of
  Lancaster*, Kindle edn (London, 2021), p. 119.
13 Turner, *Chaucer*, p. 124.
14 Simon Walker, 'Katherine [*née* Katherine Roelt; *married name*
  Katherine Swynford], Duchess of Lancaster (1350?–1403)', *Oxford
  Dictionary of National Biography*, www.oxforddnb.com, accessed
  22 November 2021.
15 Carr, *The Red Prince*, p. 120.
16 Ibid.
17 Ibid., p. 142.
18 Ibid.
19 On the contemporary echoes of medieval misogyny, see for example
  Natalie Hanna, 'From Chaucer to Trump, Sexist Banter Has Been
  Defended as Entertainment for 600 Years', *The Conversation*,
  12 October 2017, https://theconversation.com.

20 Jean de Meun, *The Romance of the Rose*, in *Woman Defamed and Woman Defended: An Anthology of Medieval Texts*, ed. Alcuin Blamires et al. (Oxford, 1992), pp. 148–66 (p. 162).

21 Since Richard tore down Sheen Palace in his grief over Anne's death there on 7 June 1394, it is presumed that the 'F version' of the *Legend*'s prologue was written before that date.

22 *The Athenaeum*, 2405, 29 November 1873, pp. 698–9.

23 Close Roll 219, 3 Ric. II, m.9 d, in Crow and Olson, eds, *Chaucer Life-Records*, p. 343. Anna Fore Waymack has also assembled translations of the legal documents related to the Chaumpaigne case and a useful bibliography in her online 'De raptu meo' resource: http://chaumpaigne.org, accessed 6 February 2020.

24 Christopher Cannon, '*Raptus* in the Chaumpaigne Release and a Newly Discovered Document Concerning the Life of Geoffrey Chaucer', *Speculum*, LXVIII/1 (1993), pp. 74–94 (p. 81). See pp. 78–81 of Cannon's article for a fuller discussion of the problem, as well as Henry Ansgar Kelly, 'Meanings and Uses of *Raptus* in Chaucer's Time', *Studies in the Age of Chaucer*, XX (1998), pp. 101–65; and Caroline Dunn, *Stolen Women in Medieval England: Rape, Abduction and Adultery, 1100–1500* (Cambridge, 2012), pp. 18–51.

25 Cannon, '*Raptus*', p. 92.

26 John Gardner, *The Life and Times of Chaucer* (New York, 1977), pp. 252–3.

27 For the 1993 discovery of a King's Bench quitclaim, see Cannon, '*Raptus*'. For a 2019 discovery of new documents, see Sebastian Sobecki, 'Wards and Widows: *Troilus and Criseyde* and New Documents on Chaucer's Life', *English Literary History*, LXXVI (2019), pp. 413–40.

28 For transcriptions and translations of the documents in question, as well as scholarly discussion of their significance, see the special issue of *Chaucer Review* dedicated to the discovery ('The Case of Geoffrey Chaucer and Cecily Chaumpaigne: New Evidence', *Chaucer Review*, LVII/4 (2022).

29 '[A]nte finem termini inter eos concordati absque causa racionabili *et* licencia ipsius Thome recessit in servicium ipsius Galfridi'; Euan Roger, 'Appendix 2: Transcriptions and Translations', *Chaucer Review*, LVII/4 (2022), pp. 440–49 (pp. 441–2).

30 Euan Roger and Sebastian Sobecki, 'Geoffrey Chaucer, Cecily Chaumpaigne, and the Statute of Laborers: New Records and Old Evidence Reconsidered', *Chaucer Review*, LVII/4 (2022), pp. 407–37 (p. 427).

31 Larry D. Benson et al., eds, *The Riverside Chaucer,* 3rd edn (Oxford, 2008), p. 1086.

32 Ibid., p. 1087.

33 Paul Strohm, *Chaucer's Tale: 1386 and the Road to Canterbury,* Kindle edn (New York, 2014), p. 46.

34 Gavin Douglas, *Aeneid,* in *The Middle Scots Poets,* ed. A. M. Kinghorn (London, 1970), pp. 162–3.

6 Conflict

1 Helen Carr, *The Red Prince: The Life of John of Gaunt, the Duke of Lancaster,* Kindle edn (London, 2021), pp. 170–71.

2 'The Letter of John Ball', in *Medieval English Political Writings,* TEAMS, ed. James M. Dean (Kalamazoo, MI, 1996), available online at https://d.lib.rochester.edu, accessed 9 November 2021.

3 Paul Christophersen, 'The Englishness of *Sir Gawain and the Green Knight*', in *On the Novel: A Present for Walter Allen on His 60th Birthday from His Friends and Colleagues,* ed. B. S. Benedikz (London, 1971), pp. 46–56 (p. 48).

4 London, British Library MS Sloane 2435, f. 85r.

5 Carr, *The Red Prince,* p. 161.

6 Derek Pearsall surmises that 'Chaucer was quite an important person in 1380 . . . at the height of his public career and, to some extent, at the height of his career as a poet, too' (*The Life of Geoffrey Chaucer: A Critical Biography* (Oxford, 1992), p. 128).

7 Paul Strohm, *Chaucer's Tale: 1386 and the Road to Canterbury,* Kindle edn (New York, 2014), p. 96.

8 Ibid., pp. 123–4.

9 Martin M. Crow and Clair C. Olson, eds, *Chaucer Life-Records* (Oxford, 1966), pp. 1–2, 147, and the table displaying the payments of Chaucer's exchequer annuities, at pp. 308–13. See also Pearsall, *The Life of Geoffrey Chaucer,* p. 146.

10 Pearsall, *The Life of Geoffrey Chaucer,* p. 146.

11 E. M. Dadlez, 'Truly Funny: Humor, Irony, and Satire as Moral Criticism', *Journal of Aesthetic Education,* XLV/1 (2011), pp. 1–17 (p. 9).

12 *MED,* s. v. *estat.*

13 Jill Mann, *Chaucer and Medieval Estates Satire* [1973] (Cambridge, 2009), p. 3.

14 Marion Turner, *Chaucerian Conflict: Languages of Antagonism in Late Fourteenth-Century London* (Oxford, 2006), p. 5.

15 Mann, *Chaucer and Medieval Estates Satire*, p. 17.

16 On lapses of clerical chastity in the Middle Ages, see Katherine Harvey, *The Fires of Lust: Sex in the Middle Ages* (London, 2021), pp. 86–98.

17 Helen Cooper, *Oxford Guides to Chaucer: The Canterbury Tales*, 2nd edn (Oxford, 1996), p. 38.

18 Ibid., p. 292. On later medieval English antisemitism, see Anthony Bale, *The Jew in the Medieval Book: English Antisemitisms, 1350–1500* (Cambridge, 2006).

19 John Foxe, *The Acts and Monuments of John Foxe: With a Life of the Martyrologist, and Vindication of the Work*, ed. George Townsend, 8 vols [1843–9] (New York, 1965), vol. IV, p. 249; cited in William Kamowski, 'Chaucer and Wyclif: God's Miracles against the Clergy's Magic', *Chaucer Review*, XXXVII/1 (2002), pp. 5–25 (p. 23 n. 2).

20 John Dryden, 'Preface', *Fables Ancient and Modern Translated into Verse from Homer, Ovid, Boccace, and Chaucer, with Original Poems* (London, 1700), p. *C.

7 Bawdy Chaucer

1 Helen Carrel, 'Food, Drink and Public Order in the London *Liber Albus*', *Urban History*, XXXIII/2 (2006), pp. 176–94 (pp. 179–80). See also Andrew Prescott, 'Brembre, Sir Nicholas (d. 1388)', in *Oxford Dictionary of National Biography*, www.oxforddnb.com, accessed 17 October 2022.

2 Paul Strohm, *Chaucer's Tale: 1386 and the Road to Canterbury*, Kindle edn (New York, 2014), p. 184.

3 Martin M. Crow and Clair C. Olson, eds, *Chaucer Life-Records* (Oxford, 1966), pp. 268–9.

4 Ibid., p. 145.

5 '[A]d quamplura ardua et urgencia negocia nostra'; ibid., pp. 61–4.

6 Ibid., pp. 329–30.

7 The Issue Roll entry specifies that the annuity is to be paid in two equal portions distributed twice annually: once at the end of Michaelmas and once at the end of Eastertide ('ad terminos Sancti Michaelis et Pasche per equales porciones'); ibid., p. 329. See also Marion Turner, *Chaucer: A European Life* (Princeton, NJ, 2019), p. 372.

8 Crow and Olson, eds, *Chaucer Life-Records*, pp. 348–63.

9 Ibid., p. 402.

10 Ibid., pp. 477–8.

11 Both versions of the prologue to the *Legend of Good Women* include a reference to 'al the love of Palamon and Arcite/ Of Thebes' (LGW F. 420–21, G. 408–9), which is almost certainly a reference to *The Knight's Tale* – the F prologue was likely written sometime between 1382 and 1394, and the G prologue in or after 1394. See '*Legend of Good Women, The*', *The Oxford Companion to Chaucer*, ed. Douglas Grey (Oxford, 2003), available online at www.oxfordreference.com, accessed 2 September 2022.

12 Larry D. Benson et al., eds, *The Riverside Chaucer*, 3rd edn (Oxford, 2008), p. 7.

13 Alan J. Fletcher, 'The N-Town Plays', in *The Cambridge Companion to Medieval English Theatre*, ed. Richard Beadle and Alan J. Fletcher (Cambridge, 2008), pp. 183–210 (p. 208 n. 31).

14 *The Riverside Chaucer*, p. 8.

15 For an overview of such assessments, see Marion Turner, *Chaucerian Conflict: Languages of Antagonism in Late Fourteenth-Century London* (Oxford, 2006), pp. 2–5.

16 See Susan E. Phillips, *Transforming Talk: The Problem with Gossip in Late Medieval England* (University Park, PA, 2007); and Carissa M. Harris, *Obscene Pedagogies: Transgressive Talk and Sexual Education in Late Medieval Britain* (Ithaca, NY, 2018).

17 Helen Cooper, *Oxford Guides to Chaucer: The Canterbury Tales*, 2nd edn (Oxford, 1996), p. 94.

18 Medieval scribes appear to have been equally confounded. Some of them noted that they could not find any more of the tale or that Chaucer had not written any more. Others took a more creative approach and appended a moralizing conclusion (or even a series of moralizing interpolations) to the text. And at least 25 manuscripts have included the *Tale of Gamelyn* (a romance) as a kind of second, rather less bawdy, tale told by the Cook.

19 See Mary C. Flannery, 'Looking for Scribal Play in Oxford, New College MS 314', *New College Notes*, 12 (2019), www.new.ox.ac.uk, accessed 6 March 2023.

20 Nigel Saul, *Richard II* [1997] (New Haven, CT, 1999), pp. 400–404.

21 Crow and Olson, eds, *Chaucer Life-Records*, p. 535.

22 Ibid., pp. 547–9.

8 Becoming Chaucerian

1 See the marketing for *The Fabliaux: A New Verse Translation*, trans.
  Nathaniel C. Dubin (New York, 2013), www.norton.com, accessed
  4 September 2022.

2 Peter Ackroyd, *The Canterbury Tales: A Retelling* (New York, 2009).

3 Sam Jordison, 'How Chaucer Weaves High-Minded Poetry
  with Low Comedy', *The Guardian*, 18 September 2018,
  www.theguardian.com.

4 Published as Anne Middleton, 'Loose Talk from Langland
  to Chaucer', *Studies in the Age of Chaucer*, XXXV (2013),
  pp. 29–46 (p. 29).

5 George Shuffelton, 'Chaucerian Obscenity in the Court
  of Public Opinion', *Chaucer Review*, XLVII/1 (2012), pp. 1–24
  (p. 2).

6 *Urban Dictionary*, s.v. *Read Some Chaucer*, www.urbandictionary.
  com, accessed 4 September 2022.

7 John M. Bowers, 'The Canterbury Interlude and the Merchant's
  Tale of Beryn: Introduction', in *The Canterbury Tales: Fifteenth-
  Century Continuations and Additions*, TEAMS, ed. John M. Bowers
  (Kalamazoo, MI, 1992), https://d.lib.rochester.edu, accessed
  9 September 2022.

8 George Whetstone, *The Right Excellent and Famous Historye of
  Promos and Cassandra*, in *Shakespeare's Library*, ed. W. C. Hazlitt
  (New York, 1965), pp. 6, 215.

9 See Lars Engle, *Shakespearean Pragmatism: Market of His Time*
  (Chicago, IL, 1993), pp. 136–7 (though the putative etymological
  link between 'quaint' and 'cunt' has been called into question
  by a number of scholars).

10 See Philip S. Palmer, '"The Progress of Thy Glorious Book":
  Material Reading and the Play of Paratext in *Coryat's Crudities*
  (1611)', *Renaissance Studies*, XXVIII/3 (2014), pp. 336–55 (p. 340).
  The phrase appears in a reference to an encounter with a courtesan
  and is likely a joking allusion to *The Miller's Tale*.

11 *The cobler of Caunterburie, or an inuective against Tarltons newes
  out of purgatorie* (London, 1590), STC (2nd edn), 4579, p. 2.
  The Scholar's Tale is the exception: it tells the tale of two lovers
  fleeing a family feud who are first separated when pirates attack
  their ship but who are ultimately reunited.

12 'An Apologie of Poetrie', in *Orlando Furioso in English heroical verse,
  by Iohn Haringto[n]* (London, 1591), STC (2nd edn) 746.

13 'F. B. to his very louing friend, T. S.', in *The Workes of our Antient and Lerned English Poet, Geffray Chaucer, Newly Printed* (London, 1598), STC (2nd edn) 5077.

14 Richard Brathwait, *A Comment upon the Two Tales of Our Ancient, Renovvned, and Ever-Living Poet Sr Jeffray Chaucer, Knight* (London, 1665).

15 *Canterbury Tales: Composed for the Entertainment of all Ingenuous Young Men and Women at Their Merry Meetings* (London, 1687).

16 John Dryden, *Fables Ancient and Modern Translated into Verse from Homer, Ovid, Boccace, and Chaucer, with Original Poems* (London, 1700).

17 Ibid., p. *Cv.

18 William Lipscomb, *The Canterbury Tales of Chaucer, Completed in a Modern Version* (Oxford, 1795).

19 Ibid., p. viii.

20 For an overview of eighteenth-century criticism concerning Chaucer, see David Hopkins and Tom Mason, *Chaucer in the Eighteenth Century: The Father of English Poetry* (Oxford, 2022).

21 Daniel Defoe, 'Not Fit for Modest Persons to Read, 1718', in Derek Brewer, ed., *Chaucer: The Critical Heritage*, vol. 1: *1385–1837* (London, 1978), p. 174.

22 Lord Byron, 'List of the different Poets, dramatic or otherwise, who have distinguished their respective languages by their productions' [1807], in *The Complete Miscellaneous Prose*, ed. Andrew Nicholson (Oxford, 1991), p. 3.

23 Steve Ellis, *Chaucer at Large: The Poet in the Modern Imagination* (Minneapolis, MN, 2000), p. 46.

24 Ibid., p. 47.

25 Ibid. On children's adaptations of the *Wife of Bath's Tale*, see Lucy Fleming, 'Unknowing Readers Reading Rape: A Brief Look at Children's Versions of Chaucer's Wife of Bath's Tale', guest post for the blog of the Swiss National Science Foundation Eccellenza project 'Canonicity, Obscenity, and the Making of Modern Chaucer (COMMODE)', published 8 September 2021, https://commode. hypotheses.org/215, accessed 13 September 2022. Fleming notes that the rape is often reframed or toned down in these children's adaptations.

26 Ellis, *Chaucer at Large*, p. 49.

27 This tendency to view Chaucer as a 'congenial' figure, and one with whom scholars and readers felt they could identify, has been laid out

most comprehensively in Stephanie Trigg, *Congenial Souls: Reading Chaucer from Medieval to Postmodern* (Minneapolis, MN, 2002).

28 Shuffelton, 'Chaucerian Obscenity', pp. 20–21.

29 'Kiln Theatre presents *The Wife of Willesden*, adapted by Zadie Smith', https://kilntheatre.com, accessed 13 September 2022.

SELECT BIBLIOGRAPHY

The following items represent only a tiny fraction of the vast body of writing related to Chaucer's life and work, but they are a useful starting point for those readers eager to form a closer acquaintance with the medieval poet and his world.

Manuscripts

Cambridge, Cambridge University Library MS Gg.4.27
Kew, The National Archives, Public Record Office, E/101/411/9
London, British Library, MS Cotton Nero A.x/2
London, British Library, MS Sloane 2435
Oxford, Bodleian Library MS Fairfax 16
Philadelphia, University of Pennsylvania MS Codex 902
San Marino, CA, Huntington Library, MS EL 26 C 9

Editions of Chaucer's Texts

Benson, Larry D., et al., eds, *The Riverside Chaucer*, 3rd edn
    (Oxford, 2008)
The Canterbury Tales, ed. William Caxton (Westminster, c. 1483),
    STC (2nd edn) 5083
*The Workes of our Antient and Lerned English Poet, Geffray Chaucer, Newly
    Printed*, ed. Thomas Speght (London, 1598), STC (2nd edn) 5077
The Workes of our Antient and Lerned English Poet, Geffrey Chaucer,
    ed. Thomas Speght (London, 1598), STC (2nd edn) 5079

Translations, Adaptations and Imitations of Chaucer's Texts

Ackroyd, Peter, *The Canterbury Tales: A Retelling* (New York, 2009)
Brathwait, Richard, *A Comment upon the Two Tales of Our Ancient,
    Renovvned, and Ever-Living Poet Sr Jeffray Chaucer, Knight*
    (London, 1665)
*Canterbury Tales: Composed for the Entertainment of all Ingenuous Young
    Men and Women at Their Merry Meetings* (London, 1687)

The Cobler of Caunterburie, or an Inuective Against Tarltons Newes Out of Purgatorie (London, 1590), STC (2nd edn) 4579

Dryden, John, *Fables Ancient and Modern Translated into Verse from Homer, Ovid, Boccace, and Chaucer, with Original Poems* (London, 1700)

Lipscomb, William, *The Canterbury Tales of Chaucer, Completed in a Modern Version* (Oxford, 1795)

Studies on Chaucer

Akbari, Susanne Conklin, and James Simpson, eds, *The Oxford Handbook of Chaucer* (Oxford, 2018)

Bestul, Thomas H., 'Did Chaucer Live at 177 Upper Thames Street? The Chaucer Life-Records and the Site of Chaucer's London Home', *Chaucer Review*, XLIII/1 (2008), pp. 1–15

Boitani, Piero, and Jill Mann, eds, *The Cambridge Companion to Chaucer*, 2nd edn (Cambridge, 2008)

Bowers, John M., ed., *The Canterbury Tales: Fifteenth-Century Continuations and Additions*, TEAMS (Kalamazoo, MI, 1992)

Brewer, Derek, *Chaucer and His World* (Cambridge, 1978)

—, ed., *Chaucer: The Critical Heritage*, vol. 1: *1385–1837* (London, 1978)

Brown, Peter, ed., *A New Companion to Chaucer* (Oxford, 2019)

Butterfield, Ardis, *The Familiar Enemy: Chaucer, Language, and Nation in the Hundred Years War* (Oxford, 2009)

Cannon, Christopher, '*Raptus* in the Chaumpaigne Release and a Newly Discovered Document Concerning the Life of Geoffrey Chaucer', *Speculum*, LXVIII/1 (1993), pp. 74–94

Cooper, Helen, 'Chaucerian Representation' and 'Chaucerian Poetics', in *New Readings of Chaucer's Poetry*, ed. Robert G. Benson and Susan J. Ridyard (Cambridge, 2003), pp. 7–50

—, *Oxford Guides to Chaucer: The Canterbury Tales*, 2nd edn (Oxford, 1996)

Crow, Martin M., and Clair C. Olson, eds, *Chaucer Life-Records* (Oxford, 1966)

Ellis, Steve, *Chaucer at Large: The Poet in the Modern Imagination* (Minneapolis, MN, 2000)

Gray, Douglas, ed., *The Oxford Companion to Chaucer* (Oxford, 2003), available online at www.oxfordreference.com

Hopkins, David, and Tom Mason, *Chaucer in the Eighteenth Century: The Father of English Poetry* (Oxford, 2022)

Horobin, Simon, *The Language of the Chaucer Tradition* (Cambridge, 2003)

Mann, Jill, *Chaucer and Medieval Estates Satire* [1973] (Cambridge, 2009)

Mead, Jenna, 'Chaucer and the Subject of Bureaucracy', *Exemplaria*, XIX/1 (2007), pp. 39–66

Middleton, Anne, 'Loose Talk from Langland to Chaucer', *Studies in the Age of Chaucer*, XXXV (2013), pp. 29–46

Pearsall, Derek, *The Life of Geoffrey Chaucer: A Critical Biography* (Oxford, 1992)

Roger, Euan, 'Appendix 2: Transcriptions and Translations', *Chaucer Review*, LVII/4 (2022), pp. 440–49

—, and Sebastian Sobecki, 'Geoffrey Chaucer, Cecily Chaumpaigne, and the Statute of Laborers: New Records and Old Evidence Reconsidered', *Chaucer Review*, LVII/4 (2022), pp. 407–37

Seal, Samantha Katz, 'Chaucer's Other *Wyf*: Philippa Chaucer, the Critics, and the English Canon', *Chaucer Review*, LIV/3 (2019), pp. 270–91

Shuffelton, George, 'Chaucerian Obscenity in the Court of Public Opinion', *Chaucer Review*, XLVII/1 (2012), pp. 1–24

Sobecki, Sebastian, 'Wards and Widows: *Troilus and Criseyde* and New Documents on Chaucer's Life', *English Literary History*, LXXXVI/2 (2019), pp. 413–40

Staley, Lynn, *Following Chaucer: Offices of an Active Life* (Ann Arbor, MI, 2020)

Strohm, Paul, *Chaucer's Tale: 1386 and the Road to Canterbury*, Kindle edn (New York, 2014)

Trigg, Stephanie, *Congenial Souls: Reading Chaucer from Medieval to Postmodern* (Minneapolis, MN, 2002)

Turner, Marion, *Chaucer: A European Life* (Princeton, NJ, 2019)

—, *Chaucerian Conflict: Languages of Antagonism in Late Fourteenth-Century London* (Oxford, 2006)

Wimsatt, James I., ed., *Chaucer and the Poems of 'Ch'*, TEAMS, revd edn (Kalamazoo, MI, 2009)

Medieval Literature and Culture

Bale, Anthony, 'From Translator to Laureate: Imagining the Medieval Author', *Literature Compass*, V/5 (2008), pp. 918–34

'Ball, John', attrib., 'The Letter of John Ball', in James M. Dean, ed., *Medieval English Political Writings*, TEAMS (Kalamazoo, MI, 1996)

Barrington, Candace, and Sebastian Sobecki, eds, *The Cambridge Companion to Medieval English Law and Literature* (Cambridge, 2019)

Bennett, Michael J., 'The Court of Richard II and the Promotion of Literature', in *Chaucer's England: Literature in Historical Context*, ed. Barbara Hanawalt (Minneapolis, MN, 1992)

Blamires, Alcuin, et al., eds, *Woman Defamed and Woman Defended: An Anthology of Medieval Texts* (Oxford, 1992)

Boccaccio, Giovanni, *The Decameron*, trans. G. H. McWilliam, 2nd edn (London, 1995)

Cantor, Norman F., *In the Wake of the Plague: The Black Death and the World It Made* (New York, 2001)

Carr, Helen, *The Red Prince: The Life of John of Gaunt, the Duke of Lancaster*, Kindle edn (London, 2021)

Carrel, Helen, 'Food, Drink and Public Order in the London *Liber Albus*', *Urban History*, XXXIII/2 (2006), pp. 176–94

Christopherson, Paul, 'The Englishness of *Sir Gawain and the Green Knight*', in *On the Novel: A Present for Walter Allen on his 60th Birthday from His Friends and Colleagues*, ed. B. S. Benedikz (London, 1971), pp. 46–56

Classen, Albrecht, ed., *Handbook of Medieval Culture: Fundamental Aspects and Conditions of the European Middle Ages*, 3 vols (Berlin, 2015)

Cohn, Samuel, 'After the Black Death: Labour Legislation and Attitudes towards Labour in Late-Medieval Western Europe', *Economic History Review*, n.s., LX/3 (2007), pp. 457–85

Coppack, Glyn, *Medieval Merchant's House, Southampton* (London, 2003)

Douglas, Gavin, *Aeneid*, in *The Middle Scots Poets*, ed. A. M. Kinghorn (London, 1970)

Dunn, Caroline, *Stolen Women in Medieval England: Rape, Abduction and Adultery, 1100–1500* (Cambridge, 2012)

Fletcher, Alan J., 'The N-Town Plays', in *The Cambridge Companion to Medieval English Theatre*, ed. Richard Beadle and Alan J. Fletcher (Cambridge, 2008)

Foxe, John, *Ecclesiasticall History Contayning the Actes and Monumentes of Thynges Passed in Euery Kynges Tyme in This Realme*, 2nd edn (London, 1570)

Galbraith, V. H., ed., *Anonimalle Chronicle, 1333 to 1381* (Manchester, 1927)

Green, Monica H., 'The Four Black Deaths', *American Historical Review*, CXXV/5 (2020), pp. 1601–31

Harris, Carissa M., *Obscene Pedagogies: Transgressive Talk and Sexual Education in Late Medieval Britain* (Ithaca, NY, 2018)

Harvey, Katherine, *The Fires of Lust: Sex in the Middle Ages* (London, 2021)

Hector, L. C., and Barbara F. Harvey, eds and trans., *The Westminster Chronicle* (Oxford, 1982)

Hoccleve, Thomas, *The Regiment of Princes*, ed. Charles R. Blyth, TEAMS (Kalamazoo, MI, 1999)

Kelly, Henry Ansgar, 'Meanings and Uses of *Raptus* in Chaucer's Time', *Studies in the Age of Chaucer*, 20 (1998), pp. 101–65

Lydgate, John, *The Siege of Thebes*, ed. Robert R. Edwards, TEAMS (Kalamazoo, 2001)

Mertes, Kate, *The English Noble Household, 1250–1600: Good Governance and Politic Rule* (Oxford, 1988)

Minnis, Alastair, *Medieval Theory of Authorship: Scholastic Literary Attitudes in the Later Middle Ages*, 2nd edn (Philadelphia, PA, 2010)

Olson, Glending, 'Making and Poetry in the Age of Chaucer', *Comparative Literature*, XXXI/3 (1979), pp. 272–90

Orme, Nicholas, 'Childhood and Education', in *Geoffrey Chaucer in Context*, ed. Ian Johnson (Cambridge, 2019), pp. 219–29

Phillips, Susan E., *Transforming Talk: The Problem with Gossip in Late Medieval England* (University Park, PA, 2007)

Saul, Nigel, *Richard II* (New Haven, CT, 1997)

Shuffelton, George, ed., *Stans Puer ad Mensam*, in *Codex Ashmole 61: A Compilation of Popular Middle English Verse*, TEAMS (Kalamazoo, MI, 2008)

Spindler, Erik, 'Flemings in the Peasants' Revolt, 1381', in *Contact and Exchange in Later Medieval Europe: Essays in Honor of Malcolm Vale*, ed. Hannah Skoda, Patrick Lantschner and R.L.J. Shaw (Woodbridge, 2012), pp. 59–78

Staley, Lynn, ed., *The Book of Margery Kempe*, TEAMS (Kalamazoo, MI, 1996)

Tatton-Brown, 'Excavations at the Custom House Site, City of London, 1973', *Transactions of the London and Middlesex Archaeological Society*, XXV (1974), pp. 117–219

ACKNOWLEDGEMENTS

To write a book about Chaucer's life is to embark on a project that is as daunting as it is thrilling. To attempt to write such a book while the world is in the grips of a global pandemic, however, is virtually impossible, unless one is fortunate enough to have the support and encouragement of family, friends and colleagues. I am therefore extremely grateful to all those who lent me their support along the way, especially Anthony Bale, Sarah Jane Brazil, Az Brown, Helen Cooper, Kristen Haas Curtis, Daniel DiCenso, Lucy Fleming, Daryl Green, Carissa Harris, Annette Kern-Stähler, Simone Marshall, Zoë Pagnamenta, Daniel Sawyer, Devani Singh, Stephanie Trigg, Daniel Wakelin, Katie Walter and Anne Yardley. Kathleen Flannery and Jean Judge kindly read through a very early draft of the book, and their feedback was invaluable. Deirdre Jackson and Michael Leaman were insightful readers of the draft manuscript; their comments, and the expertise of Alex Ciobanu and Amy Salter, have vastly improved this book. Any remaining errors or infelicities are entirely of my own making. Much of the preliminary research for this book was supported by the European Commission (Marie Sklodowska-Curie Fellowship), the University of Oxford, and a visiting fellowship at Magdalen College, Oxford, to whom I remain extremely grateful. My thanks also to the University of Bern and the Swiss National Science Foundation (Eccellenza Professorial Fellowship), whose support enabled me to complete the project. Last but certainly not least: this book never would have been written had I not had the good fortune to work with two truly exceptional Chaucerians. The late Colin Wilcockson made me fall in love with Chaucer more than twenty years ago – for that I owe him much love and heartfelt thanks. And it was Helen Cooper who first showed me how rich Chaucer criticism could be – for that she will always have my deepest gratitude and admiration.

PHOTO ACKNOWLEDGEMENTS

The author and publishers wish to express their thanks to the sources listed below for illustrative material and/or permission to reproduce it. Some locations of artworks are also given below, in the interest of brevity:

Badminton House, Gloucestershire: p. 42; Beinecke Rare Book and Manuscript Library, Yale University, New Haven, CT: p. 32; Bibliothèque nationale de France, Paris (MS Français 25526, fol. 106v): p. 138; Bodmer Lab, Université de Genève (CC BY-NC 4.0): p. 19; British Library, London: pp. 20 (Royal MS 17 D VI, fol. 93v), 77 (Royal MS 14 E IV, fol. 244v), 80 (Royal MS 14 E IV, fol. 10r), 107 (MS Harley 4425, fol. 114r), 121 (MS Sloane 2435, fol. 85r); Geograph® Britain and Ireland: p. 18 (Michael Garlick, CC BY-SA 2.0); courtesy Dr John Wyatt Greenlee: pp. 6, 8, 9; © John Harding, the Sheela Na Gig Project: p. 148 (*right*); The Huntington Library, Art Museum, and Botanical Gardens, San Marino, CA (MS EL 26 C 9): pp. 96 (fol. 72r), 98 (fol. 72r), 134 (fol. 148v), 158 (fol. 153v); The J. Paul Getty Museum, Los Angeles (MS 100, fol. 26v): p. 149; The National Gallery, London: pp. 90–91; University of Pennsylvania Libraries, Philadelphia (MS Codex 902, fol. 75r): p. 55; Westminster Abbey, London: p. 93; Wikimedia Commons: pp. 17 (JRennocks, CC BY-SA 4.0), 34 (Geni, CC BY-SA 4.0), 148 (*left*; William Ellison, CC BY-SA 4.0).

INDEX

Page numbers in *italics* refer to illustrations